Also by Jenny Cockell

ACROSS TIME AND DEATH

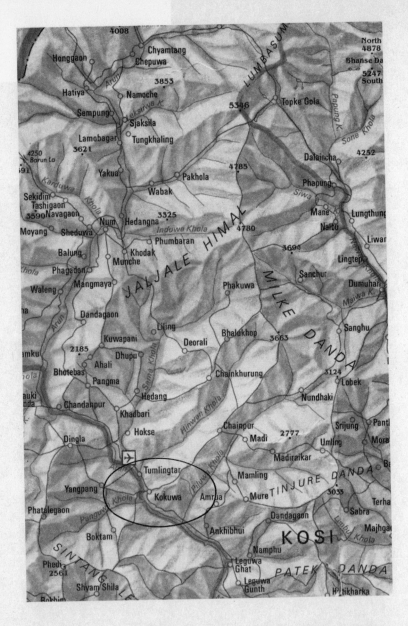

A detail from a map of Nepal showing Kokuwa which Jenny feels is the nearest town to Nadia's hillside village. Jenny believes that Nadia's village is approximately 3 miles north-east of Kokuwa on the track to Chainpur (see page 128). (© Nelles Maps, Germany)

JENNY COCKELL
Past Lives, Future Lives

A FIRESIDE BOOK
Published by Simon & Schuster

Acknowledgements

All life is interconnected, which means that it is hard to know where to begin thanking people who helped with this book. So I thank everyone, especially those who allowed me to use their names or experiences, and, in particular, Anthea Courtenay for her invaluable editing.

FIRESIDE
Rockefeller Center
1230 Avenue of the Americas
New York, NY 10020

Copyright © 1996 by Jenny Cockell
Published by arrangement with Judy Piatkus Publishers Ltd
First published in Great Britain in 1996
All rights reserved,
including the right of reproduction
in whole or in part in any form.

FIRESIDE and colophon are registered trademarks
of Simon & Schuster Inc.

Manufactured in the United States of America

1 3 5 7 9 10 8 6 4 2

Library of Congress Cataloging-in-Publication Data is available.

ISBN 0-684-83216-X

The cartoon on page 92 is reproduced with kind permission of *The Mail on Sunday*.

Contents

Foreword

British publisher's note about Jenny Cockell

We published Jenny Cockell's first book *Yesterday's Children* in 1993 and it quickly became a bestseller around the world. Readers in America (where it was published under the title of *Across Time and Death*), France, Germany, Italy, Spain, Holland, Sweden, Norway and Denmark have all been amazed and captivated by the book and its message.

Jenny's story is believed to be one of the most powerful proofs of the existence of reincarnation. It has been taken up enthusiastically by radio and television everywhere and is now regularly mentioned in books and articles on the afterlife.

Across Time and Death is also a supreme example of a mother's love overcoming insuperable obstacles. From childhood, Jenny felt that she had lived before. She believed she was an Irishwoman called Mary who had died in the 1930s. Jenny lived with a deep sense of guilt because she knew she had abandoned her 'children' before they were old enough to look after themselves. Her book traces her search for proof of her former life and for the children she had left behind. While she was writing it, Jenny met one of her 'sons', Sonny, now in his seventies. But it was not until after publication that she was able to find the actual cottage in Malahide, outside Dublin, where Mary Sutton had lived and bring together the rest of the children, who had been separated at Mary's death. It was through Jenny's perseverance and the media coverage generated by her book that the family was reunited.

We hope you enjoy reading *Past Lives, Future Lives*, and that you will want to read *Across Time and Death*. Jenny is a brave and sincere person, with extraordinary powers. We are proud and delighted to be her publisher.

Judy Piatkus
London, 1996

Introduction

Although this is my second book, it is not entirely a sequel to the first. In many ways it is the book that I have always wanted to write and for which I have collected information over many years. In it I hope to bring together a sense of the continuity of past, present and future, based on my experience of past-life memories and visions of the future. Time is not just the present, for the present is only a tiny fraction of our existence. We are more than the reflections that we see in our mirrors, and far more than the separate isolated creatures that we may feel ourselves to be.

Ever since my early childhood, I have had memories of other, past lives, as well as premonitory dreams and waking glimpses of the future. One of my past lives in particular haunted me – my life as Mary Sutton, a mother of eight children who died after childbirth in a Dublin hospital in 1932. In my book *Yesterday's Children*, I have told the story of my search for Mary's family and how I was actually able to trace and meet some of the children from whom Mary was parted at her death.

Also as a very young child I discovered that most people are unable to remember past lives. Because to me these memories felt quite normal, I believed that they must be a common experience and I was shocked when I realised that reincarnation was not accepted by everyone. I also learned not to talk about my other psychic experiences and premonitions, for fear of being thought 'different'.

For me, the cathartic effect of tracing my past-life family was extremely positive. It was like emerging into the light after years of walking in shadows, and it gave me the motivation to look further into other areas of psychic experience, such as precognition.

Perhaps because of the intensity of concentration required in my past-life search, or perhaps because I had developed a greater conscious awareness of the continuity of the soul through many lives, my sporadic visions of the future made a sudden leap, and were no longer restricted to my lifetime. Now they seemed to be involving me in a future life. At a time when I was still trying to trace Mary's children, I found myself having a totally clear sense of myself as a child in the next century. Once I had completed my search for the past, I knew that I must start exploring the future.

I was aware that this new search would be difficult to explain and even harder to verify, but just as I had felt compelled to find the family from my past, I knew that the future could not be ignored, that I had to look further into this extraordinary experience and gain some clearer understanding. This book tells the story of my research into the future, as far ahead as the twenty-third century.

In any precognitive vision there are clues, however slight, that relate to the surrounding environment; they include general living conditions, social structure and events in the world at large. Piecing together my own glimpses of the future, I found enough consistent features to be able to take an overall view from the fragments available, a view which I am now sharing with others.

We trust our perception to provide a picture of everything around us. Our senses create a window to the outside world, and what we experience subjectively creates our view of reality. It can be quite a surprise to find that our awareness is not always identical with that of other people. In a society in which conformity is rewarded from childhood on, anyone whose experiences do not conform to the generally accepted norm can be fearful of being thought different. But there is more to life than just what we can see or touch or hear with our ordinary senses.

Probably everyone has had some experiences that have directed and affected the course of their lives – perhaps an odd coincidence that has led to a total change of direction, or a feeling that warns one to avoid a particular course of action that later turns out to have been potentially damaging. Most of these occurrences are put down to intuition rather than labelled 'paranormal'. Yet more people than would perhaps like to admit to it have occasional insights into the future. In ancient civilisations such visions were taken very seriously; modern Western culture seems inclined to ignore them or explain them away. But some of us are unable to ignore what we see, and know from experience that it is possible to glimpse tomorrow.

Today, there are also growing numbers of people who are willing to describe their glimpses into a realm beyond death in what are known as near-death experiences. Their descriptions are surprisingly consistent and provide vital clues to the nature of existence. If we accept their memories relating to a time between lives, perhaps we should try to understand the driving forces that lead us to return to physical life.

For those like myself who accept reincarnation as a certainty, the future is relevant to every one of us, not just for the sake of our children and grandchildren but for ourselves in future lives. If we are to return, what kind of world will we be returning to? Everyone is now aware of the environmental damage that humankind is inflicting on its only habitat, but how can we know which forms of pollution will be easiest to control or resolve, and what sort of long-term damage we may have to contend with?

The only way to find out more about the world we live in and our place in it, present and future, is to ask questions. This is logical, and even if the questions sometimes seem outrageous they can be useful, since along the way we can take some small steps towards finding some of the answers. This book is an attempt to ask and answer a few of the questions relating to our long-term future.

CHAPTER 1

Building Blocks

The road towards past and future

Psychic events have always felt so much like an ordinary part of my life that I still find myself objecting when people refer to me as though I am special or different. I certainly don't feel different; I make mistakes and worry and forget to do things, just like everyone else, and have to apologise when I get it wrong. But I do remember that it was once quite difficult to reconcile my own inner experience with the outlook of people around me, especially when I was a very small child.

I was born in Barnet, Hertfordshire, on 10 July 1953; a year later my family moved to a new housing area not far away on the edge of St Albans. My father was a rising electronics designer, my mother a housewife, and I had two brothers. We enjoyed a semi-rural setting, as the estate nestled against open countryside and woodland which I loved to walk through. I also enjoyed watching the last steam trains from my window and their distant carriage lights outlining the dark horizon on winter nights. My pleasure in both the countryside and the steam trains was coloured by their echoes of an earlier existence.

From earliest childhood I had memories that I knew were of

my previous lives; the most dominant was the life of Mary Sutton which I have written about in *Yesterday's Children* and which haunted me for many years. But I could remember at least two other past lives in some detail and had occasional recall of several others. I also often had dreams of the near future which invariably came true.

The first time I had any idea that my view of reality was different from other people's was when I started going to Sunday school. I was nearly four, not yet at day school, and had as yet no real understanding of life outside my home. It felt strange sitting on the floor at the front of a crowd of children in the old scout hut, a musty-smelling building which lacked proper heating. Here I day-dreamed, taking in my surroundings rather than listening to what was going on.

I did prick up my ears one day, however, when someone began talking to us about death and what happened afterwards. Miss Barrand, the district nurse who ran the Sunday school, had introduced a solidly built man in a suit who was talking about heaven. I agreed with quite a lot of what he was saying, but was very concerned that he made no mention of past lives. I assumed that everyone had such memories, and had already begun to wonder why other people didn't discuss them. As I listened to this man, I couldn't understand how he could talk about subjects like death and heaven without including other lives, past or future.

This was something of a crisis point for me, and when I got home I asked my mother about it. Although at that time she didn't believe in any life after death, she was sympathetic as she explained to me that reincarnation was a belief and not an accepted fact. Soon after this I found out that other people, particularly other children, were disbelieving or at least puzzled when I talked about past lives or indeed about my dream glimpses of the future. I learned to be selective about whom I spoke to about these experiences, and began to keep some things to myself.

As a small child, I would spend some time each day in a withdrawn meditative state; most children day-dream, of course, but this was a very regular feature of my life. It was my gateway to a spiritual and psychic awareness that I continued to think of as very normal and everyday. It also became my escape mechanism from stress at home, where life was often darkened by my father's moods.

My father was a fit, imposing giant of a man. He was very quiet most of the time, though when he did feel communicative he had a curious knack of explaining complex ideas in a few succinct words. He had very high ideals, but sometimes he would be troubled and moody for long spells, and at these times we learned to avoid him whenever possible, for his anger could be terrifying.

I remember my early childhood fairly easily; I can recall sitting in my pram, and later conversing with adults before I was old enough for school. But my later childhood years, particularly between eight and thirteen, have been partially supressed; my mother and surviving brother are unable to recall those years properly either. I do remember my older brother Michael receiving a number of severe beatings, as did my younger brother Alan, too, on occasion. Selective memory is a powerful protector of the self-image, but I do know that I was sometimes afraid.

Once, when I was about seven, I went downstairs after bedtime to say something to my mother. My father shouted at me not to stand too near the oil stove in case I burned myself – which made me jump so that I did indeed burn my wrist badly on the stove. I was so afraid of punishment that I didn't cry out. Back in bed, the pain was so bad that I couldn't sleep, but fear made me stifle my tears and I pushed my face into the pillow so that nobody would hear me cry. The hot metal of the stove imprinted a small clover leaf design on my left wrist, and the scar remained for many years.

When Michael started school his teacher was worried because he was so far ahead of the rest of the class. In common with several of my relatives, including an uncle who was invited to assist for a year with the maths for the Apollo space project, he was discovered to have a genius-level IQ. When I went to school, by contrast, the teachers were concerned because I appeared to be slow. I had learned to escape from the unhappy atmosphere at home by day-dreaming, and of course this made it difficult for me to concentrate on work. I was a quiet child and easily upset, which was not helped by the negative attitude at my first school. Assuming that most teachers were like my father, I feared punishment if I made a mistake and was terrified when they shouted at anyone in the class.

When I was eight a routine IQ test showed that I was in fact much brighter than my school work had led everyone to believe. I was moved into a top group, where I tried to remain alert for long enough to concentrate on my work. But I was so afraid of getting things wrong that I used to go through my answers over and over again, compulsively checking and rechecking, which of course slowed me down.

Although I was quiet I always made friends fairly easily, both at school and Sunday school. However, until the age of seven the people I regarded as my closest friends were different: these were the two 'imaginary friends' who appeared to me when I was in a trance. Nobody else could see them, but to me they were totally real. They looked quite solid, and I knew they were people who had actually lived, though I never thought of them as ghosts – if I had, I would probably have been quite frightened.

They were friends, and I felt they had been together as friends in life. One was a young man, perhaps in his early twenties; I felt he had been a soldier in the Second World War. His constant talking and joking could at times be a bit irritating and I preferred to talk with his companion, an older, quieter man with a lot of patience.

I regularly had long conversations with these two: we communicated mentally, and although I don't remember our talks in detail they were very comforting and important to me. We didn't talk about everyday things but about feelings and matters of a more spiritual nature. The older man would advise me on how to be, and how not to let others try to change the person inside; he would try to build up my confidence by telling me about his own experiences.

I was very upset when one day my friends told me they would

not be able to return. It was in the playground at primary school and we were all three sitting on a wall surrounding a small planted patch of ground. When I asked why they were leaving, they said something about it being time to move on and time for me to grow up some more, which I didn't really understand. They didn't leave straightaway but sat on the wall while the teacher blew the whistle; they were still there when I looked back as we filed into the classroom. The last I saw of them, they were sitting on the wall, waving at me and smiling.

I missed them deeply. It was the first time I had experienced any sort of loss or grief, and I tried to call them back a few times – but without success. After that I did begin to grow up a bit; I spent less time in trance, and concentrated more on the world that everybody could see.

When I was nine, as well as going to Sunday school I began to attend Bible study classes on Thursday evenings, mainly because my older brother and a friend also went. I soon became disenchanted with the limited view of conventional religion that we were taught. I had very clear ideas of my own and felt unable to compromise. Later I looked into other religions, and I was delighted when the school curriculum was altered to include comparative religion. But although I found more in Eastern beliefs to match my own views, I still found all religious teaching constricting. I tried to fit in, but I couldn't see God as a separate or overseeing entity; my idea of 'God' was more like an energy that included all living things and of which we were all a part.

I wasn't keen on many childhood games; what I really enjoyed was tidying and cleaning! My toys were kept neatly in boxes, which I labelled as soon as I could write, and my clothes were always carefully folded and stacked. This was partly so that it would be easy to move out when my parents decided to separate – an event which I anticipated and which occurred in my early teens – but I also took pleasure in the act of cleaning itself, and in looking after my part of the home.

I also enjoyed looking after my brothers, and eventually I cared for a host of small, unwanted animals. My collection started with a few stick insects given to me by a friend of Michael's, and went on to include several slow-worms, a whole lot of mice, and some snakes and unusual small mammals. One summer I managed to help out at a small zoo next to the Roman part of St Albans – the ruins of Verulamium. This housed animals under the care of the naturalist Graham Dangerfield, including Goldie the golden eagle who achieved fame by escaping for a time.

At home things did not improve. Despite our careful behaviour, my brothers and I were constantly attracting our father's wrath. By the time I was nine he had developed a pattern of discipline that was unfair, brutal and demoralising. We would be lined up after a minor misdemeanour and questioned in turn, though we were usually too terrified to speak. My father would then decide who was guilty, and beat the selected culprit.

One of the worst times was when I ate five marshmallows from an open packet in the larder and my father decided that Michael was responsible. I remember that beating especially vividly as it should have come to me, and I felt so very guilty. Afterwards I went to confess to Michael, and tried to apologise as he lay writhing on his bed in tears of agony. We had been very close until then, but this single event strained our relationship severely for a long time to come.

Some people might wonder why my mother didn't take us away much sooner, but at that time life was very difficult for single parents. There was a strong chance that, if she tried to leave and had a problem supporting us, we could be taken into care; that was a prospect she couldn't face.

Some people outside the family could sense my fear and recognised me as a potential victim, so that I became a target for bullying and abuse at school. But by the age of ten I had started to learn how to fight back. Although I could do nothing at home, I was not going to let anyone else frighten me. As a result I became aloof, distant and cautious. I also tried to protect my brothers. I took part in a series of mock fights with boys from among my friends, one of them accidentally ending in a bleeding nose. As a result I gained a reputation for toughness, and was able to protect my brothers just by being with them.

My school work improved as I began to 'wake up' for more of the time, enough for me to gain a grammar school place, but I did not begin to achieve anything like my potential ability until I was thirteen, when my parents finally separated. This was a huge relief. However, by the time my mother, brothers and I moved out, I had fallen into a pattern of deep depression; there would be months on end during which I found it hard to concentrate, alternating with bouts of tremendous, almost obsessive enthusiasm – usually for a personal project of a creative or artistic nature.

For a while we lived with friends of my mother's and it was two years before we finally settled in a house of our own. My life from fifteen onwards was totally different from my early childhood. Although my mother was both teaching and studying, the atmosphere was relaxed. Our home was often full of visitors, and there always seemed to be time to talk.

I hated secondary school; I found it hard to make friends there and felt unhappy and isolated. However, I began to develop a full social life outside. I joined youth groups and a folk dance group; I enjoyed anything to do with the countryside and exercise, from charity walks to canoeing, and went on camping or activity trips whenever I could.

At sixteen I went to study for my A-levels at a college of further education, where I spent two very happy years. The environment was much more positive and relaxed and I found it easier to make friends. I even found myself better able to get on with my father. On Sundays I used to go to a jazz club where he played, and between sessions we were able to talk. Gradually I began to understand his own bleak childhood and the inner pain that gave rise to his anger, and was able to forgive him.

I was beginning to open up all round, and it was at this time that my interest in various psychic phenomena began to grow. I was finding it easier to talk to friends about my past-life memories and gauge their attitudes towards a range of paranormal experiences. Partly because I disliked the idea of being different, my aim in discussing these phenomena was to help to normalise the paranormal. I do not believe that people who are psychic are different from others; we all have different abilities, and this happens to be one of them.

My own psychic experiences increased, becoming far more prevalent in this supportive environment than they had been in my stressful pubescent years. Memories of past lives, particularly that of Mary Sutton, recurred regularly, as did flashes of the future. I realised that many of my shorter-term premonitions turned out to be accurate, and began taking notice of my visions of the more distant future.

One of these really worried me. It took the form of an extremely vivid, complex and detailed dream in which I saw myself in my mid-thirties going through a crisis involving financial disasters and family worries. During one very clear scene I saw that I would have two blond children, despite being dark-haired myself, and I was sure that one was a girl; I saw the worried expression on my face as we all arrived somewhere in an estate car. At the same time, I knew that after this bad patch was over something would happen that would change my life, after which I would have no more major worries.

I was also aware of an increase in a number of minor phenomena, often in the form of telepathy. One day, for instance, I returned home to find my mother searching for something in drawers and cupboards. I joined in her search and eventually found a tape measure, which I handed to her. Only then did we realise that she had not said a word about what she was looking for.

It probably helped that my mother was always very much in tune with her children. When Michael had a cycle accident one day, he returned home to find my mother worried and wanting to know what had happened. So, a little later, when I was given a lift home but the car's fan belt broke, I remembered to think, 'I'm all right Mum, but I'll be a bit late.' When I got back my mother was still awake but not worried; she said, 'I knew you were all right – you told me.'

Most instances of telepathy occurred spontaneously, but when I was around seventeen I began to experiment with it more deliberately by sending mental messages. For example, I found that a dog will do what you 'think wish' it to do – such as 'come here, then go and scratch at the door' and so on – whereas a cat would embark on the activity, then stop and look me in the eye and refuse to go on!

I also discovered that if I had a strong connection with a person I could will them to act out a short sequence, though it took a long time to get through to them. I began by trying single-action mental commands, like willing someone to scratch their ear. When they did, I decided that this could be a coincidence and proved nothing, so I next tried a detailed and complex sequence of actions on a particular person. The experiment was highly successful in that the person followed exactly the sequence of actions and manner I had been concentrating on, but I immediately realised that it was a very wrong thing to do. After carrying out my mental suggestions to the letter, my unwitting victim looked very confused and upset. I felt guilty about this for years afterwards and later wrote to apologise: I never attempted anything of this kind again.

I did draw some conclusions from these experiments. It would seem that animals are aware of telepathy; a dog may understand and do what you ask simply to please you, while cats too may understand but don't have the same need to please. People, however, are not usually conscious of mental requests, and can be extremely upset to find themselves acting out of character without knowing why.

It seems that animals can also communicate with us, if we are receptive. My first pet snake, a grass snake, was given to me by a friend when I was sixteen, because it had been very nervous of people and was known to bite. Although it remained nervous of other people, we slowly built up a trusting relationship, and it never bit anyone again.

One Saturday morning I had a premonition that I didn't at first associate with my pet. I was wide awake and the vision was very strong and vivid. I saw a friend of my mother's and her children, and I felt as if I myself was dead, and under water – strangely, this feeling was not frightening but totally calm and loving. It was puzzling, because I was sure I wasn't about to die.

That afternoon my mother's friend called on us unexpectedly and I introduced her children to the snake. When I put it back into its tank it slid lifelessly into the shallow water trough, and I realised that it had died quietly in my hands. I believe that the snake had known it was going to die and wanted me to understand that this was nothing to be sad about. The loss of my pet was tempered by the tremendously uplifting experience we had shared in my vision, and I had no need to mourn.

After that I would sometimes know when people were going to die. There didn't seem to be any pattern to these knowings, and they didn't occur with everyone, but if I foresaw a death it always happened. I never told anyone about these premonitions.

After passing my A-levels I spent three years training in London as a chiropodist. During this period I lost contact with several good friends who had gone on to various universities. Lacking the confidence to consider university myself, or to aim at more ambitious career options, I had picked a course that was well within my abilities and would guarantee me a qualification for a secure career.

Commuting to London by train each day while studying very hard took its toll. Although I performed very well in the exams, I became extremely tired and withdrawn and, for a while, quite severely depressed. Towards the end of my second year at college, when I was nineteen, I entered into a relatively brief but ill-advised relationship which was dangerously reminiscent of my early experiences as a victim of manipulation and bullying. Though the relationship lasted little more than a year it served to revive and reinforce fears that survived both from my childhood and from my most recent past-life memory.

A few years later, after my marriage, someone told me that the man concerned had moved to our area. When a man with similar features and build parked near our house, I jumped to the conclusion – wrongly – that he had hunted me down, and I was terrified. Coincidentally, we got ourselves a big Alsatian dog about this time, which suddenly seemed a good idea! A little later I took up the martial art of Aikido to help me to restore some inner confidence. I found it very beneficial and kept it up for seven years, until my daughter was four.

While my disastrous relationship was at its worst I was for some time disturbed by a particular psychic image, which appeared frequently at times of stress in my life. What I was seeing was my own face, not as it was then at the age of twenty-one, but an old and white-haired me, looking back at me across time. At first I saw it reflected in mirrors, then superimposed on other faces, even on posters. Now I understand that this image was actually sent as a kindly reassurance, as if my future self were trying to send me some comfort, but at the time it bothered me.

I needed to find someone I could discuss it with, but there seemed to be very few people with similar experiences to whom I might turn. Then my mother came across a psychic who was highly recommended by a friend, and I went to see her. Her name was Mary; she was a gentle and very normal lady, separated from her husband and the mother of a teenage son.

One of the first things she did was to give me her ring to hold. I immediately started seeing very vivid mental pictures. I saw Mary walking a dog by a river, and told her that the dog was black with longish curly hair. I saw a Dutch house where I knew her friends lived, by what looked like a river, and then her ex-husband, standing apart from a group of chatting people while he brooded and wished to be alone.

Mary asked me if the ring was warm; although I hadn't noticed it, it had actually become quite hot. She had asked me to hold the ring because she sensed that I was psychic, and the ring becoming warm would normally have been the first indication; my ability to 'see' so easily was a bonus. She then showed me a photograph of the dog – identical to the one I had seen – and told me about her Dutch friends who lived by a canal. She told me that I had described everything accurately, and explained that this ability to see images by holding an object was called psychometry.

After this Mary went on to 'see' for me, and we discussed the vision of myself that had been so troubling. It was a great comfort to feel free to talk about such an experience without embarrassment. I was very reassured to meet, at last, someone else who had experiences like mine. As for the psychometry, it had never occurred to me that I could tap psychic information on purpose – this was fun! After that I would practise it whenever the opportunity arose.

Psychometry is a way of tuning in to an object that has been owned and handled, usually by one person, in order to access feelings, sensations and pictures which are somehow imprinted on the object. This is not as far-fetched as it may sound. It is increasingly accepted that human beings are electromagnetic systems and that we can affect the functioning of electrical and electronic items such as voltmeters. It doesn't take a great deal of imagination to see how we may also leave on objects some sort of electromagnetic imprint, perhaps a little like the sound and pictures recorded electromagnetically on a video or audio cassette.

I enjoy practising psychometry from time to time simply for the pleasure of it; it is very much like watching part of a film or listening to a short piece of music. For a time I quite often did it for friends. The results are a little variable but sometimes I see very detailed pictures of the past, present and, more rarely, the future. I find it works best when the owner of the object has a strong personality or if the object has been used for a specific purpose.

I hold the item gently, and relax and concentrate for a few minutes. It takes a while to develop a light trance and let go enough to feel sensations emanating from the object. Usually something happens, even if it is only a slight change in my mood relating to the feelings of the owner of the item rather than my own. Sometimes I see snapshot pictures. Like most psychic visions these are usually mental images, rather like memories but with a more persistent quality. I may just as easily sense sounds or smells. On one occasion I could smell creosote, and the owner of the ring I held laughed and said that her husband kept obsessively creosoting their fence.

Usually I would be given something common like a ring or bunch of keys, but antiques were my favourite, especially weapons or items that originally had a purpose and were therefore handled regularly and with concentration. Old items can feel very strange; when handling these I experience a falling sensation which took me by surprise the first few times it happened. I have found that the older the object, the longer the 'falling time', so that sensation gives me an idea of its age. If the pictures are very vivid, or the emotional detail intense, I sometimes find myself shivering. This tends to worry people who are watching, but is actually not unpleasant.

After leaving college in 1974 I worked briefly near Croydon in Surrey, where I met Steve, who became my husband. We looked for a home in Northamptonshire and in 1976 moved into a small but enchanting cottage. Here I began working for the Northamptonshire Health Authority. Alongside the demands of ordinary life, marriage and eventually two children, psychic experiences continued to occur regularly.

Some of these insights were quite ordinary – like the lady who walked into my chiropody clinic one day and to whom I remarked, 'You've been doing a lot of knitting lately.' It immediately seemed a silly thing to have said, but she responded that for weeks she had been knitting dozens of toys for a charity bazaar. Then she looked at me and said, 'How did you know?' I wasn't sure what to say.

In my early married life I practised psychometry from time to time. At a party in Buckingham, a friend gave me some car keys belonging to her next-door neighbour, whom I didn't know. I felt very strange at first, as if I were shooting up into the air – like being in a lift but surrounded by open space, which was extremely disorientating. This made sense when the owner of the keys told me that his father used to take him up in his hot-air balloon, which of course would travel straight up.

I also saw his car with the bonnet up, parked on his driveway. There were car parts lying all around and he seemed to be quite agitated. 'No,' he said. 'That has never happened – the car is in good condition.' But later it was reported to me that a week or so after the party he had had some major problem with the car, and that his father-in-law offered to help him do the job at home rather than opt for an expensive garage bill. He was half-way through, surrounded by car parts, when he remembered what I had said.

Another fairly typical example of psychometry occurred at a local steam and vintage vehicle fair in 1984. Amongst the stalls was a display of antique swords for sale. When I touched one I saw an image of a cavalry officer, so I asked the stallholder if it was a cavalry officer's sword. He said it was, and jumped to the conclusion that I knew something about the weapons. I had to explain that I knew nothing at all about swords, but that the sword itself held its own history. He was understandably sceptical, but out of interest handed me a swordstick and asked me to tell him what I could about it. I then described a white-haired gentleman of about sixty, who had a small tailored beard and a terrific sense of humour. The surprised stallholder confirmed that this was the acquaintance who had previously owned the swordstick.

I still had visions and flashes both of my past lives and of future events. One future vision which, perhaps surprisingly, bothered me very little, happened in my late twenties when I foresaw my own death as an old woman. It wasn't upsetting; it wasn't like Mary, who had died young, alone and in pain, or like another life I could recall which ended early and also involved an unresolved separation. There was some sadness at leaving the family, even though they were all grown up with families of their own. But there was no sense of fear.

Telepathy was the most consistent psychic occurrence to happen spontaneously. One day, while visiting a friend with my children, I was hit by an emotional shock wave which came from outside myself. I knew something was terribly wrong with a family member and left for home straightaway. I was relieved when my husband arrived back safely. Then I telephoned my mother; she was all right, but immediately started to give me news of my younger brother. No, he hadn't had an accident, but his progressively difficult marriage had reached a crisis that day. He had moved out and was in a very emotionally charged state, particularly about his children.

From then on I realised that my link with Alan was such that it explained many past, though usually less strong, psychic surges I had experienced in connection with him. From then on, if I experienced something similar I would check the clock and he would later confirm that he had been going through some event or panic at that time.

In 1986 my brother Michael was fatally injured in a gliding accident. At the time of the accident, Alan was telephoned first. My mother was on holiday and I was out for the day with my family, so Alan had the added worry of trying to locate everyone. At the exact moment when he received the call (for some reason I checked the clock and so did he) my family and I were in a service station on the M1 past Sheffield, and I was just about to sit down with a cup of coffee. Suddenly the whole room seemed to spin and I tripped into a seat, spilling some of the coffee. I was shaking and felt like crying. I told Steve that something terrible had happened, but it was not until we returned home that we found what it was.

I later discovered a similar link with my son. One of the haunting memories of my previous life was a sense of having deserted my children, and as a result I never liked leaving my children alone. As they grew older it became a little easier, and when my son was a teenager I didn't have too much of a problem about going off to attend a course on podiatry; he had his own front door key. However, during the second afternoon I suddenly became mentally aware of him. I knew immediately that he had forgotten his key and wondered whether he would go on down to the farm where he had a casual job egg collecting – a very smelly, dirty task – without changing out of his school clothes.

I turned to the person next to me and said, inappropriately, 'My son has forgotten his key!' I noted the time, which was about when he was due to arrive home. After a few seconds the anxiety resolved and I felt that all was well. When I got back it transpired that my son had forgotten his key but, rather than wear his school clothes in the chicken-house, had got hold of some shorts and a tee-shirt which happened to be on the washing line.

With some people whom I know well I am now able to recognise a 'signature', so that when I sense a feeling or emotion from outside myself it is usually – though not always – easier to interpret. I can sometimes tell when someone is reading a letter I have sent them. My friends have got used to my asking what they were doing at a particular time of day on such-and-such a date. Occasionally I can feel when a friend is writing a letter to me or about to phone – this last is of course a very common experience among people who don't necessarily think of themselves as psychic.

It is strange, though, that one of my most powerful telepathic experiences was concerned with people with whom I had no connection, and I still have no idea why it happened. At the time of the Falklands War in 1982 I had been practising Aikido for about a year, and I had learned that a light meditative, yet focussed, state of mind would make the techniques more effective. This is the same frame of mind that I use in psychic practice, so it may have been partly responsible for what happened next.

I was halfway though a particular throw when I suddenly became very dizzy and had to sit down. I felt that I was in a ship, trapped in a small corridor with about four men. It looked rather like the interior of a submarine, which was intensified by a horrible feeling of claustrophobia. The ship was on fire, and the doors at each end of the corridor were sealed to keep out both fire and water. There was no way out, and the men were trapped.

For about fifteen minutes I was sharing the last moments of these people whom I didn't know, and they were terrified. The fear left me when I felt them die, but the shock remained with me for considerably longer. Several people came over to ask if I was all right, and I told them what I was feeling and what I had seen. Next day we heard that HMS *Sheffield* had been sunk the previous evening. The facts of the news report could not convey the terror that for some inexplicable reason I had been caused to share.

Steve started a haulage business in 1979 and for a while all went well. He was careful and never took a full wage while the business was building up; I worked part-time after our son was born, and our finances were just about manageable. The first indication of a problem came around 1982 when I tried to look at our future, using cards as a focus for my intuition. To my dismay I kept seeing things going wrong, financial crisis and terrible emotional strain.

I couldn't believe that we could ever be in such a dire situation. At the time, I didn't connect it with that vivid dream of disaster that had so worried me at the age of sixteen. I thought that my method must be at fault and gave up looking at our own future for a while. However, by 1983 – the year our daughter was born – the start of the recession was hitting the building industry. One of the first casualties was haulage, particularly the type of small tipper business that Steve had begun to build up. Over the next three years everything turned out quite disastrously, just as I had foreseen. In addition, the Health Authority chose this moment to cut back on part-time hours, and although I looked for private clients my practice was slow to build up. It was a very worrying and difficult time, and I became quite ill. Eventually we had to give up the trucks, knowing that it would take many years before we would recover financially.

During these years there came a day when I found myself arriving by car at the place of my dream twenty years earlier. Although I knew that this meant the start of severe crises, which turned out to be personal – family – and health-related – it was in some ways a relief to know that it had arrived. Because I also knew that when it had passed, although things would be difficult, they were ultimately going to improve.

This improvement was connected with my discovery of the family of Mary Sutton, and resolving the anguish that had remained with me from that past life. From about 1980 onwards it had become increasingly important to me to find out about my past-life family and trace the children whom I felt responsible for deserting. This took nearly ten years. I began slowly by making notes of my memories, and became increasingly obsessed by my researches; I actually started writing *Yesterday's Children* before the story was complete. The turning point in my life that I had foreseen in my dream coincided with my tracing Mary's actual family and discovering a new sense of calm that I had never known before.

It was just after I had received proof that Mary Sutton had been a real person that I had my first vision of a future life – the life described in Chapter 8. In fact, I believe now that I had flashes of this earlier life before then, but I was too obsessed with my search into the past to take any notice. It is as though I have had to clear up the past and discover a sense of self-forgiveness before I could turn to the future and begin to explore my own future lives.

In early childhood I believed that everyone could remember past lives, gain glimpses of the future and experience the feelings of others through means such as telepathy. As an adult I have learned that most people lose touch with this sense of connectedness with others. I feel that it may be time for us to start to consider ourselves in a new way, other than as totally separate individuals.

Telepathy is just a reminder that we are all connected to each other; we are connected to both the past and future, too. Nothing happens in isolation: every event is intricately interwoven with everything else that is happening around us and to everybody else. We may think that the choices we make in life only affect ourselves, but everything we do affects other people and future events.

CHAPTER 2

Visions of Past and Future

Growing experience

The first time I had a vision of the far-distant future, two hundred years ahead, was in the early 1980s. It stands out very clearly in my memory, for on that day I saw the past, the present, and the near and distant future, all as part of the same experience. Since then, the major part of what I saw has been confirmed, apart from the distant future which is yet to come – and as time goes on, aspects of that future are becoming more likely. What made the experience especially useful was that it was witnessed by someone who also vividly remembers the events of that day.

As well as using psychometry I had already had some very vivid visions of the past which arose spontaneously at places with a long history. In 1978 Steve and I went to visit some friends who lived in a little cottage by a stream in a village near Whipsnade. When we arrived, our friend Sue was in the kitchen. It was dusk and beginning to get cool, and she said something about lighting the living room fire.

I was standing near the living room door, and glanced through the doorway at the fireplace. I was just about to say, 'But the fire is already lit,' when something about the room made me feel a need to enter. I took in the scene. The fire, fuelled with large logs, was burning well. There was a farm-style wooden table in the middle of the room, very much in keeping with Sue's taste; it was laid for six with what appeared to be pewter plates and antique cutlery, and no cloth or napkins. There were candles standing on it, in simple but attractive holders. I wondered who the other guests were to be.

I was about to suggest drawing the table further from the fire as the two seats at the back would become too warm, when I happened to look at the windows. There were two windows in the wall to my left, and there was something very odd about them. Through one came the kind of light one might expect on a dull day; the other, which was further from the table, showed that it was dusk outside.

Saying nothing, I turned back into the kitchen, where Sue was looking at me with a quizzical frown. I turned round and re-entered the living room. The table with its settings and candles was no longer there, the fire was unlit, and dusk was showing through both windows.

This time when I returned to the kitchen Sue asked, 'What is going on?' I told her what I had seen. As a friend she knew that this kind of thing happened to me and mainly wanted to know if my vision had been of the past or the future. All I could say was that it felt like the past. Sue wasn't altogether surprised; she too had felt odd things in that cottage.

Something similar occurred at the bluejohn mines of Nidderdale in north Yorkshire which we visited during a camping holiday in the summer of 1981. When we went in, I was fascinated to watch four or five men on ladders and ropes working in the great cavern. They continued to chip away at the rock without stopping to glance at the few tourists.

On our way out, I commented to Steve that the men who were still working were using the old methods. He looked at me a little blankly and I pointed to the display outside, showing photographs of men working in the traditional way. Only then did I see the caption beneath it, which stated that this mine was no longer worked. The penny dropped: I was the only one to have seen the miners. There was nobody there – only echoes of the past.

Heather, my daughter, has shared some of my experiences. My first visit to Warwick Castle was in 1978. Making my way to the tower from the chapel, I heard a buzzing noise and felt odd and giddy; I took it to be the start of a migraine, which I sometimes suffered from. When I reached the tower, there was a man in an ancient style of dress, sitting at a desk studying charts.

This visit of ours took place before the owners of the castle employed people dressed in period costume to entertain visitors, but he looked so real that I assumed he was somebody dressed up for some reason. After a while he got up and went towards a set of bookshelves, where he disappeared. Even this didn't strike me as odd; I assumed he had merely walked through a door next to the shelves. Immediately after leaving the tower myself I felt normal again – no more buzzing noise and no giddiness. I turned to someone and commented on the noise, blaming the fluorescent lights; the reply was, 'What noise?' No one else had heard the buzzing – and no one had seen the man in costume.

Many years later, when I returned to the castle with Heather and an old friend, I learned that other people had seen him too. It was always the same man; he had been identified as Sir Fulke Greville, the first Baron of Warwick, who had been murdered in 1628. This time, my daughter too felt something odd. As we walked through one recently opened room I suddenly felt frightened and uncomfortable. I was aware that the feeling was somehow caused by the place, and I didn't mention it because I didn't want to upset Heather. But she turned to me and expressed the very same discomfort and fear, which she too knew was to do with the place. A guide told us that the room had been a dungeon long ago; we must have been picking up the despair of the prisoners from those ancient times.

These types of experience are very like psychometry, except that instead of holding a small object, the same sense is achieved by standing within an area or room that has somehow been imprinted with past events. Using psychometry, my awareness is usually on a more subtle level. But sometimes I have a rare experience of total reality, in which all my senses seem to be functioning as though I am actually living the experience.

One occasion when I had that three-dimensional sense of reality was when I was holding a valuable antique Samurai sword belonging to a friend who taught Aikido. As I held it in my hands I felt exactly as though I was moving into the past. It was as if I was standing barefoot in the sand – I could actually feel it between my toes; I felt myself turning and moving with the sword, finally bringing the blade down to cleave a large melon. (Afterwards I was told that cleaving a melon was traditionally considered a great feat of Samurai swordsmanship, since melons have a tendency to roll!) I was aware that I was sharing the experience of the original Japanese owner at sword practice, as if I had somehow been superimposed on him.

I then went on to contact other memories locked within the sword, piece by piece, up to the present day when I found myself accurately describing the personality of the sword's current owner. Occasions where the detail is so complete are few. But another experience was even more remarkable.

Around 1981, I had got into the habit of dropping into an antique-*cum*-junk shop in an old building in Moat Lane, Towcester. I went there not just to look for bargains, but also to look into the history of objects for sale, using psychometry.

The owner of the shop, Peter Harris, was a friendly, middle-aged man with a passing resemblance to Father Christmas. He noticed me handling the objects and asked me what I was doing. Somewhat embarrassed, I told him about my experiments with psychometry. Peter was sceptical but interested; he asked me a lot of questions, and then asked if he could test me. Still rather self-conscious, I agreed, and he got me to hold some pieces of a chess set whose previous owner he knew, though I did not. He told me nothing about this person, but I was able to tell him that it had been a woman, and gave him a fairly detailed description of her which I 'felt' through the chess figures.

Surprised and intrigued, Peter wanted to know more, and

asked whether I could see the past, present and future at will. Up until then I had never really tried, and I was both curious and a little nervous about the possibility. Normally when I used psychometry I would see the present, although when I was handling something very old I might see the past, as in the case of the Samurai sword. I did occasionally have visions of the future, but these just came up by chance and I had never considered consciously controlling them. Rather diffidently, I agreed to try.

We started with the present. Peter gave me the keys of his home to hold and I was able to envisage his cottage as it was then. I described it in detail, bit by bit, including a small kitten I saw darting behind a large armchair. He was pleased I had seen the kitten, which was his only companion at that time.

Peter confirmed my description of his cottage and was particularly amused when he asked me to find the stairs and I couldn't. I had seen and described a wood-panelled wall; the door to the stairs was actually in that wall, but I had not been able to see it. Peter explained that visitors often found it difficult to locate the door; it was almost camouflaged within the wood panelling, and made of similar material. My inability to 'see' the door would have been consistent with my being there physically and looking at the wall – although I was not there at all in the physical sense.

Next I tried to take the vision into the past. Peter had mentioned that he had made a number of changes to the property; I thought perhaps I could see into the past by imagining these changes being reversed. I started by deliberately visualising this reversal, slowly at first; then the images picked up speed and became spontaneous as my mind travelled back to the early days of the cottage.

I had the usual sensation of falling which accompanied my visions of the past; it felt a little like vertigo, or going down suddenly in a lift, and could be slightly disorienting. However, it was a sensation I had learned to trust when 'feeling' the age of an object. Handling a really old item, such as a piece of armour, could cause the sense of falling to last longer.

This odd feeling slowed down and stopped, and I found myself seeing a picture, rather as if I was watching a film. At first

I was slightly above the scene, and then I was looking at the cottage, somehow knowing that the period was about two hundred years ago, around the time when it was built. I described to Peter what I saw, including the occupant of the cottage, an old man, walking down the garden path with his dog, and a doctor on horseback who was riding down the road towards them.

Peter found me a piece of paper and I sketched out a map showing the cottage, the road and surrounding details, including woodland and a farmhouse with its outbuildings. There were no other buildings. Peter was happy that I had the age of the cottage about right, and was able to confirm that most of the houses in the village were built after his; the only older building was the farmhouse. But he was convinced that I had got the map quite wrong, because the road was in the wrong place.

However, some weeks later Peter told me excitedly that he had looked at some old maps in the local library and found that the drawing I had made was entirely accurate for the period. What he hadn't known was that the bridle path at the back of the cottage had once been a road, whereas the new road on the other side had not existed at the time. Now the rest of my map fell into place.

When it came to looking at the future, I was surprised to find that this was even easier and happened more instantaneously. This time I had the idea of simply imagining Peter's kitten growing up. Once I had set this in motion I had a feeling of drifting forwards, a sort of dissociated floating, which was less unsettling than the falling sensation of travelling back in time.

On the way through the years, again a slow journey at first, I saw Peter suffering a major illness and afterwards recovering and returning to work. Normally I would not consider it right to give anyone a prediction that might worry them, but there was Peter standing in front of me while I adjusted to the sensations, and expecting me to tell him something. In truth there was probably not enough time to think about what I was saying, and I was caught a little off guard, so I told him what I saw. More important, I had seen him getting better, so I knew that when the illness actually arrived he could feel assured of his recovery. I couldn't be sure when the illness would come, but one thing I was certain about was that he would still be running the business at the same premises afterwards.

In retrospect I was probably right on this occasion to tell him what I had foreseen: about a year later he suffered a major heart attack, and was in hospital and off work for a while. The lady who worked with him in the shop was very worried, and wondered whether he would be well enough to come back. But from what I had seen I was able to assure her that Peter would make a good recovery and return to work. He did indeed do so, although the business eventually closed in 1986.

After describing to Peter his future and that of the cottage I began to see the future further ahead, though still in my own lifetime. I saw the cottage empty, and knew that many other houses would stand empty and unsold. In the 1980s the area was expanding at a rate that threatened to double the population in as little as ten or fifteen years; but I saw that there would eventually be a drop both in house sales and in the local population.

My forward vision continued; it was not unlike watching a video in fast forward. I continued to describe as much as possible of what I saw, though most of it consisted of quick glimpses with patches of darkness in between. Finally, the fast-moving pictures came to an automatic halt. I knew that we were at a point in time about two hundred years ahead; I had the sensation of having travelled through the same length of time as I had done to see the two-hundred-year-old past a few minutes earlier.

This was a remarkable experience. As I looked at the new scene not only could I see the landscape, but I experienced all the sensations of actually being there. I was aware of my physical body standing in Peter's shop, but at the same time I could feel the warmth of the sun and air so clean that it was a joy to inhale. I felt that I was viewing the same area as before; however I was looking away from the direction of the village, and didn't think to see what still existed there. I was standing near a road, and could see no people or animals. I somehow knew that there were fewer people around, perhaps a lot fewer. And although I had all my senses I could hear no birds, which really bothered me.

The fields were beautifully cultivated, machine-drilled right up to the edge of the road; the height of the green crop suggested late spring, which was confirmed by the extraordinarily mild weather. The sunlight was very bright and it was easy to see into the distance. This very clear air is something I have experienced in Africa in dry conditions. But the weather in this future vision was by no means as hot as in Africa, so perhaps the clarity was the result of dryness, or simply of a lack of atmospheric pollution.

There were no hedgerows or fences. Later I reasoned that this made economic sense, as hedgerows and fences need time and labour to maintain; if there were fewer people, there would be fewer available to do such work. However, there were a number of reasonably-sized spinneys with large mature trees. They were arranged in staggered groups, presumably as windbreaks and soil erosion deterrents; the fields ran around them continuously so that they could be farmed by machine with no need to open gates or move from field to field.

What dominated the landscape was a huge, smooth-sided, rectangular structure that I took to be some kind of power- or energy-producing unit; I had an inner feeling that this was its purpose. It stood the size of a large city office block, in open countryside to the west of Northampton. The material resembled brushed aluminium and the walls were completely smooth with no visible joints. Nor was there, on either of the two sides I could see, any entrance or outside structure or car park.

In fact I had the sense that there were few or no cars. The surface of the road I stood by was beautifully smooth and consistent, like a really perfect continuously machine-laid tarmac road, but I felt that it was scarcely used. And I could see no people at all. I was left with a sense of puzzlement. There was much that needed to be understood, and I knew that I would have to try to find out more about the future.

After the shop had closed down I did not see Peter again until 1987, when we waved at each other across the busy main road, but didn't stop to talk – to my immediate regret. Then, in the spring of 1994, wanting to ask permission to use his name in this book, I managed with some effort to trace him. He invited me to visit him at his home, which I had never been to.

After parking the car nearby I surveyed the village and located the cottage without any difficulty. I knew it was the oldest building there, and backed on to open fields by a bridle path. The whole scene was quite recognisable from my visions of some nine or ten years earlier; apart from the unevenness of the land behind the bridle path, everything was exactly as I had seen it.

Peter gave me a warm welcome and asked me in. Inside the cottage a few more changes had been made, but there were no surprises. We were able to enter into an animated discussion straightaway, as though there had been no intervening time. We had a long talk, and I felt really fortunate that Peter had remembered everything about the psychometry. It is always good to have a witness to these out-of-the-ordinary events.

At the time when they happened, it was no real surprise to find that I could see the present and the past through psychometry, even if these particular visions were rather more detailed than many I had had. Seeing the near future, including Peter's illness, was the kind of thing that happened less often but was still not new to me. It did take me a bit off guard, and since then I have been less willing to look at other people's futures for fear of seeing events with a less fortunate outcome.

However, it may have been precisely because I felt off guard that my vision that day seemed to rush away to the far-off future. Although I had had brief glimpses of the distant future before, this experience totally astounded me. It felt tangible; it was so vivid and so completely unexpected that I couldn't begin to take it all in at first. I had not been trying to see far ahead, so the quality as well as the content of the vision was a shock. For a minute it felt just as though I was standing there, two hundred years into the future, breathing the air and feeling the sun on my face in that unpeopled landscape.

The high rate of accuracy in my past, present and near-future visions for the old cottage and for Peter gave me hope that what I saw of the distant future that same day might also be right. This increased the chances that my other glimpses of the future could also be right, and encouraged me to look more consciously into the possible future of the planet by exploring my own future lives.

CHAPTER 3

Unfinished Business

The case for reincarnation

Most people's concerns about past and future are related purely to their present lives. But if the energy that is the soul is not destroyed at death, if we continue and return to live in a physical body over and over again, then both the past and the future are very much a personal concern.

Because of my personal experiences, I have never had any doubt about the reality of reincarnation. It is an expression of the immortality of the soul, which never ceases to exist but after death continues to rest in an altered state, returning later in a new body to start a new life. This conforms with the law of physics that states that energy cannot be created or destroyed. The recycling of the living energy that forms each of us is continuous and repeated, so that death becomes a change rather than an end, and birth a fresh start rather than a blank sheet.

Many ancient religious beliefs encompass this philosophy, in slightly different ways; what they have in common is the consciousness that how we live will affect what happens to us after death. In Hinduism the objective is to live in such a way as ultimately to be reunited with the absolute: the universal energy,

Brahma, which is represented by the gods Brahma, Vishnu and Siva. Each life is judged by one's deeds, and it may take many, many lifetimes to reach the ultimate goal.

Buddhism has a similar objective, though with no reference to a god. It advocates following a way of life (the 'Noble Eightfold Path') whose aim is to free us from suffering and ultimately to achieve the state of Nirvana, in which we will merge with universal life and reincarnation will no longer be necessary.

It is less well known that reincarnation is an ancient and integral aspect of Judaism, and also originally of Christianity. Both the Essenes and the Pharisees, ancient sects, taught a belief in reincarnation, and it was accepted within Christianity for over five hundred years. It was only rejected, in an undemocratic and purely political move, by the Emperor Justinian at the Fifth Ecumenical Council in AD 553, after which it was regarded as heresy.

My own beliefs about the mechanisms of reincarnation tie up to some extent with those of the Eastern religions, particularly with Hinduism and Buddhism. I am certain that we are connected at some level with all life energy, and that after many lifetimes we return to the greater energy of which we are all just a part.

As my life has gone on I have found that people's attitudes towards reincarnation are becoming more open, but it is still a difficult idea for many Westerners to accept. However, there is an increasing body of research which suggests that it is a reality that can in some cases be proved. Not only do numbers of people remember their past lives, but on occasion their memories can be, and have been, backed up by external evidence. And since the mechanisms of nature – the patterns of birth, life and death – are always consistent, what is true for some people must be true for us all, whether we remember our past lives or not.

There are two main ways of demonstrating the reality of reincarnation. One is when evidence can be found to support the accounts of people who have described past lives under hypnosis. (I myself had recourse to hypnosis in my search for Mary

Sutton's past, and during my sessions recalled several other past lives that I had not remembered spontaneously.) The most convincing demonstration, however, is the increasing number of children who talk spontaneously about past-life memories from a very early age, and are able to give specific details of those lives which can be verified. (It is also possible to recall past lives through meditation or working with dreams, but the memories that these methods produce are mainly emotional in content and lack the concrete details that researchers need to help in verification.)

There are now about 2500 documented cases of children whose descriptions of previous lives have been checked out by researchers; a number of these children have been able to contact and recognise their former families. Most of the work of research and documentation has been undertaken since 1960 by Professor Ian Stevenson of the University of Virginia, and since 1979 by Dr Satwant Pasricha in India. In *Claims of Reincarnation* Dr Pasricha describes a number of cases of children mainly living on the Indian subcontinent, who have past-life memory. She has drawn some interesting statistical data from these studies.

The age at death in the previous lives was found to be consistently low. In Sri Lanka the average age at death of past-life claimants was 14, compared with a life expectancy of 61.7. In India the age at death averaged 34, compared with a life expectancy of 52.6. There was also a very high proportion of violent or sudden deaths.

The return period – that is, the time between death in the former life and birth in the current one – was found to be short in the majority of cases. In Turkey the return frequently took place in as little as nine months; in India the average return time was eighteen months, and for the Tlingit people of Alaska it was forty-eight months.

These short return times may be accounted for by the fact that the world population is continually growing. Although there are now more people on the planet than ever before, there is not necessarily more life energy. With so many new births, it may be that at the moment we are having to spend less time resting between lives than we once did. There is a considerable variation in return times among the people whose stories can be checked, but in the cases characterised by a strong memory the return period is often very short, sometimes less than a year.

Although some people describe past lives that took place fifty or a hundred years ago, we must not assume that this is the length of the gap between their lives; there may have been several other forgotten lives in the intervening period. My own main memory, Mary Sutton's life, ended twenty-one years before my birth, but there was another brief memory during the intervening years, which would make my own rest time approximately eight years between each life.

If the rest period has to adjust to the size of the population, it would be reasonable to expect an increasing number of children remembering previous lives, simply because there has been less time to forget one life before starting another. This could account for the increase in reported cases – although this could also be due to the increasing acceptability of reincarnation, which means that adults are more likely to take serious notice of children's claims.

Within the Buddhist tradition, it is interesting that the tracing of reincarnated Lamas usually occurs when the children concerned are still very young. Before his death each Dalai Lama (who is accepted as the reincarnation of the Buddha) describes where he can be found in his next incarnation, so that he may be restored to his former position. When he dies a search is made for a child in the specified area. When the right boy is thought to have been found, he is tested by being asked to identify his own previous life possessions from amongst a quantity of similar items such as small handbells and walking sticks. The present Dalai Lama is in his fourteenth incarnation and in each new life has had to pass stringent tests before being accepted and reinstated.

The same testing process is carried out for many other Lamas. One of the best-publicised recent tracings of a Lama was that of the revered senior Lama Ling Rinpoche, who died in 1984 and was recognised as being reincarnated in a boy born in 1985. The child, only twenty-one months old when found, unerringly picked items that had belonged to his former self. He even recognised and greeted former friends and demonstrated the same personality traits and mannerisms as his former self.

Lamas, however, are not expected to retain full previous-life memory into adulthood. This conforms with Dr Pasricha's research; she noted that many of the documented children began to forget their past lives at around six years old. At this age children are usually becoming actively integrated into their present environment, going to school and acquiring all sorts of new interests. So forgetting the previous life may be a part of normal development, allowing the adaptation to society that is necessary for personal development.

In fact it appears that clear memories only survive into adulthood when there is a very strong emotional tie with the past life, such as a violent death or a sense of some important issue that has not been resolved. This may be one reason why I never forgot my own unresolved previous lives – though a certain stubbornness of personality may also have been responsible.

It is curious that even very powerful recall can begin to fade when the present life becomes more insistent. In some cases this may be because the children concerned have been able to contact their past-life families. One might think that bringing the families together would reinforce a child's memories, but presumably the meeting enables them to resolve any feelings of 'unfinished business' so that the importance of the previous life diminishes. Frequently those who have been reunited with the previous-life family while still very young have gone on to forget and let go of that past life.

Because it is likely that all children retain some snatches of memory from previous lives, such things are liable to affect preferences or behaviour. Young children, typically around the age of four, may demonstrate behavioural traits that are not to do with their present environment. This should not be considered abnormal; it is a very common feature of past-life memory. Most of the children who were investigated demonstrated play activities that had some connection with the previous life – just as I enjoyed sweeping and cleaning as a small child. In addition, many suffered from fears related to their past memories, such as a fear of water following a death by drowning.

As well as acting out their memories, some of these children demonstrated skills that they had had no opportunity to learn in their current lives, including such things as knowing how to drive or speaking a foreign language. It is not unusual for children to display particular abilities without actually having complete memories of former lives; the skill itself may indeed be all that remains of the past experience, but this would certainly explain why some people develop special interests or skills at a remarkably early age.

It seems that the child prodigy in particular does not need to retain detailed past-life memories to be able to draw on a retained skill. I remember a girl at school who greatly surprised not only her audience but herself when she sang alone for the first time: her voice sounded as though she had received a full operatic training.

Music is just one of the skills that can appear in full flower in young children with little or no teaching. A supreme example was Mozart, who began his musical career when he was four and was touring Europe at the age of six. It seems very possible that such prodigies are relearning a skill rather than learning it for the first time. In a few cases there appears to be no learning process at all: the skill is simply there.

Raymond De Felitta, for example, played the piano for the first time in 1971 at the age of six; he found to his delight – and to his parents' consternation – that his fingers were 'doing it themselves'. What his fingers were doing was playing jazz in the style of the great Fats Waller, who died in 1945. 'Blind Tom' Wiggins of Georgia, though apparently educationally subnormal and with a limited vocabulary, was playing the piano like a professional from the age of four with no lessons.

Other child geniuses have included John Stuart Mill, the nineteenth-century philosopher and economist, who knew Greek at the age of three. Jean-Louis Cardiac, born in France in 1719, knew the alphabet at three and could translate Latin at four; sadly, he died at seven. The Cuban world champion chess player, José Capablanca, was playing brilliantly and winning games against adult opponents at the age of four.

Much of the recent interest in past-life research was inspired by a remarkable investigation which took place in India nearly seventy years ago. The story of Shanti Devi is perhaps the earliest case of reincarnation to be seriously investigated and widely publicised. It also includes most of the features listed in Dr Pasricha's statistics.

Shanti Devi was born in Delhi in 1926. At the age of four she started to talk about her 'other life', comparing the clothes she wore now with those she had worn 'before'. She described details of her life as someone called Lugdi who had lived in Muttra, 80 miles (130 km) away, and who died ten days after the birth of a son. Shanti asked to return to Muttra to see her family, and eventually a letter was sent to Kedar Nath Chaubey, Lugdi's widower.

Kedar Nath wrote back saying that much of what Shanti had said was true. He asked a friend in Delhi to visit the family to find out more, and eventually decided to visit Shanti himself. Shanti was nine years old when Kedar Nath visited Delhi on 13 November 1935 with his young son. During an emotional meeting Shanti Devi recognised Kedar Nath and spoke of their life together with such conviction and accuracy that he was convinced that she had indeed been his late wife, who had died in 1925 at the age of twenty-three.

As a result of the ensuing publicity a committee was formed to conduct an investigation, and it was decided to take Shanti Devi to Muttra. On arriving at the station she recognised her former father-in-law and parents amongst the crowd. She directed the carriage driver to her previous home, pointing out local landmarks on the way. Inside the house, she was able to describe the former furnishing and layout (Kedra Nath no longer lived there, and these had been changed). She looked for 150 rupees that she had hidden, and when she couldn't find them Kedar Nath admitted that he had found the money and

39

taken it. Shanti Devi expressed maternal feelings towards her previous son and reacted to all other family members with obvious recognition and affection.

This case is important because of the high proportion of correct details given and because there was an investigation before the two families met. Of the 2500 cases documented to date, only some twenty-five of the children were independently interviewed before meeting their previous-life families, which gives leeway for the suggestion that they could have learned some of the details of their past lives from these families.

Another remarkable and much more recent case which has some similar features is that of Titu Singh, born in 1986 in the village of Baad in India. He was two and a half years old when he began to talk about a previous life which ended violently with his murder. He claimed to have been Suresh Verma, with a wife called Uma and two children, Ronu and Sonu; he had owned a radio and TV shop in Agra. Initially his family was disbelieving, but eventually he convinced them enough for them to send his oldest brother to the town of Agra, 8 miles (13 km) away. There he found the shop, named Suresh Radio, and met the widowed Uma.

Titu's brother explained to Uma why he had come, and she visited his family the next day. Titu immediately recognised her and called out to his parents that his 'other family' had arrived. After talking with Uma and Suresh Verma's parents Titu's family decided to find out more. When he was about six Titu was taken to the shop in Agra, where he commented on changes that had been made, such as the presence of new shelves. He greeted Uma, and reminded her of past events in their married life; she finally accepted, with some anguish, that he was the reincarnation of her late husband. Titu subsequently recognised the two children amongst a group playing in the street.

A fascinating detail in this case is that Titu bears a birthmark on his head where he says the bullet hit him; it is in exactly the same spot as the wound located in the autopsy report on Suresh Verma. In 1992 Titu appeared in an Agra court and convinced the authorities that he was a murder victim, naming his murderer!

In a BBC documentary shown in March 1990 in the *Forty Minutes* series, Titu's two families met and were interviewed. When I saw the programme, what struck me was the difficulties involved when someone has two lives and wants to try to live them both. At the time I was engaged in trying to trace my own past-life family; I was encouraged by the programme, but very aware of the emotional problems it could bring up.

Both Shanti Devi and Titu Singh had done what I was trying to do: they had recovered that which had been lost. But it became clear that in some ways this can hold one back. Shanti Devi never married; she always felt married to Kedar Nath Chaubey, even though he had taken a second wife. Titu Singh felt strongly drawn to his past and to his previous parents, which must have made his present parents very uneasy. This sense of being pulled in two different directions is an integral part of such memories; this very tension may be one reason why the memories continue into the present.

Past-life memories that are retrieved under hypnosis do not seem to require the same sense of an unresolved past, except when used in therapy. The memories that surface during hypnotic regression have normally been forgotten because the subject has been able to let go of that former life – which I believe is what should happen. Even so, the memories that are easiest to access under hypnosis are those entailing a sense of the unresolved. Our past is a part of us, and if we consider that we have many lives then the memory of those lives must also be a part of us. This suggests that memory is not just stored in the physical brain but forms an integral part of the spirit.

Although most of the documented research has been carried out in the East, where the notion of reincarnation is culturally acceptable, more cases are now arising of Western children remembering past lives. This may be because parents today are more willing to listen to what their children tell them without belittling their statements – even if they don't necessarily believe them.

In *The Children That Time Forgot* Mary Harrison describes

how she placed an advertisement in a women's magazine asking for mothers to contact her if they had had any odd experiences with young children. She was expecting to collect light-hearted anecdotes for a book; instead she received hundreds of letters about children who reported details of previous lives. The common phrase used by the children was 'when I was here before'. The stories they told were consistent in their detail; they did not change or become embellished with each retelling, despite the youth of the children concerned.

Mary also notes that some children were able to remember the time between lives and waiting to be conceived. There was an energy barrier that was frequently described as being like a river that had to be crossed. Dr Peter Fenwick of the Institute of Psychiatry in London has carried out brainwave readings of unborn children and concluded that before birth the patterns were identical to those of an adult when dreaming, suggesting that babies dream while still in the womb. Yet our dreams are usually stimulated by experiences, past and present. In an unborn child with no present-life experiences, the mental images likely to stimulate dreams might well relate to previous lives or the time between lives.

When each of my children was born I automatically looked at them in order to see who they had been before. I had done this for friends, often quite spontaneously, for several years, so I was not at all bothered when after a little concentration I could see another face superimposed over the face of my baby. With this glimpse, as on those previous occasions, I also picked up fragmented images that related to those former lives.

Although I told Steve and my mother about the pasts I had seen for them, I never mentioned them to either of the children. I preferred to wait and see if they remembered anything for themselves and whether this would match what I had seen. In addition, I feel very strongly that children should be encouraged to develop their own points of view, so I didn't discuss my views on reincarnation and past lives with them until they were old enough to ask for my opinion and consider their own.

I saw my son as a young soldier in Europe, possibly France. At the age of two he himself used to talk animatedly about mountaineering, describing and naming mountaineering equipment. Without mentioning previous lives, I carefully asked if he thought he had ever lived near a mountain. His answer was immediate: 'No, but a friend of mine did.' I left it at that and eventually he spoke no more about climbing. A few years later he had forgotten all about the experience and now has no recall of it.

My daughter also apparently had a past life in Europe: I saw her as a grandmother in one of the Baltic states, dressed in black and surrounded by a large and loving family. As a toddler, Heather would dress as a lady by placing a shawl over her head and crossing it on her body in the style of a middle European peasant of older times. When she helped me make pastry she would twist it into shapes which reminded me of biscuits I had seen many years earlier at a Latvian festival. Because these were play activities rather than conscious memories, Heather did not associate them with a past life.

Why are a few people apparently able to remember past lives while the majority seem to forget? It is likely that most children have a fractional memory of previous lives, but normal integration into the present makes it possible for them to forget these as they grow up. This is liable to be the norm, so that adults who recall past lives are in the minority. It is extremely unusual for someone to retain a detailed memory of a previous life into adulthood; this perhaps would require a combination of an unresolved past, together with a tenacious personality.

Case studies suggest that, when memories persist, there is a strong emotional commitment to the past life. In virtually all of the child cases studied there was a sudden and premature end to the life, and a sense of unfinished business. These children may also have brought with them a strong sense of responsibility or guilt, or the anguish of separation from a loved family. They may also have a determination to remember that would explain why such children need to reinforce their memories by talking about them and re-enacting them in games.

These factors were evident in the case of Shanti Devi and

Titu Singh, particularly the sense of loss and unfinished business. They were at the root of my drive to search for Mary Sutton's family, and also featured in my other remembered lives.

The other lives that I have always remembered from childhood have affected my present life almost as much as the memories of Mary. My second most prevalent past-life memory was as a young girl in Japan. It is a life I found difficult to talk about until recently, because it too brought to the surface in me a sense of failed responsibility.

The time was around the middle of the nineteenth century (I have somehow always had an inner knowledge of when my past lives took place). I was one of the children of a well-to-do family living near a small fishing village on the north-west coast of the southern island of Japan. Further north was a larger community where I was not permitted to travel alone. We lived in an attractive home on the hillside above the village and we children were not allowed to mix with the working people whose small dwellings crowded close to the shore, near the clusters of fishing boats. I don't recall being required to work and my life was very calm and ordered, if rather restricted.

When I was about seventeen my father took me to the town to the north. We travelled by boat; it was bigger than the tiny fishing vessels of the village, but nevertheless crowded. I was to meet an influential man whom my father had arranged for me to marry, so the trip was quite an excitement. But when we finally reached our destination I felt uncomfortable with the place; I was not used to the crowds, and the town was far less beautiful than our hillside home.

When I met the man I was to marry, my depression was compounded. I knew he was a good match as far as the family was concerned, for he had an excellent position, but he was old and not at all attractive. While my father and the old man spoke and made arrangements, I was taken to another room. We were in a large house; I was not sure if it was my fiancé's home or whether it belonged to the family of the elderly female relative who sat with me in near-silence while the men carried out their negotiations. I had only been in the room with my husband-to-be for a few minutes, and had spoken only to answer a few polite questions about the journey. Later in the day we left and stayed somewhere else before the return trip.

My father brought me back home to prepare for the wedding. It had all been agreed and, as a dutiful Japanese daughter, I had no say in the decision. I felt frustrated and depressed; I had to do what my father wanted because to disobey would be to dishonour him. I simply had no right to refuse the marriage; my father had chosen well and struck a good bargain. But although refusal was unthinkable, deep down that was what I wanted to do. I felt ashamed that such a rebellious thought could even cross my mind, but at least I had sufficient respect for my father to hide my feelings.

Soon I was on the boat again, this time destined for my wedding. I knew that I had to go, in obedience to my father – an obedience soon to be transferred to my new husband. We were within sight of land towards the journey's end when the boat collided with a small fishing vessel; the crew of the smaller boat were too busy arguing with each other to notice that they were heading for an accident.

There was a fairly substantial thud. The passengers were crowded together, some standing, and on impact several of us were thrown into the water. Because I hadn't been allowed to play with the village children I had never learned to swim, but I should have been close enough to the boat to be pulled out of the water. Somehow, that isn't what happened.

I remember a brief moment of absolute panic, followed by a sense of dissociation as my body fell limply down through the water. The transition from unconscious body to a spirit free from the body went almost unregistered: I just seemed to move quite naturally into a state where there was no fear. I didn't look back to see if my body was still sinking, but was drawn towards what seemed to be an anti-clockwise swirling in the water above me. I recognised this as death and freedom, and offered no resistance as I was drawn into the vortex and peace.

Although this death enabled me to escape from a life I didn't want, I had always carried a great sense of guilt about dying then, as if I had deliberately chosen to die rather than following the path of duty and responsibility. Recently, however, I was involved in a discussion about a drowning which had happened in a very similar way. I was told that sometimes when people hit the water the shock causes them to breathe in deeply, filling their lungs with water. Weighed down in this way, they tend to sink without resurfacing.

At this point in the conversation my death in Japan flashed into my mind, and I suddenly found myself in tears. For all these years I had felt guilty and responsible for what had been purely an accident. At last I was able to forgive myself and understand that it was time to let go of the feelings that had hurt from several lifetimes ago.

Similarly, I had also felt guilty about dying as Mary, which was a major reason for my search for her family. I was finally able to go through a similar release from that guilt when I realised at last that she was in no way to blame for her death. Thus it is possible to see a pattern emerging over more than one life that expresses a continuity of the personality.

Oddly enough, probably my oldest memory in time is also the happiest. Far from being concerned with unfinished business, it is imbued with a great sense of completion and fulfilment. This memory has been with me from childhood.

I was a young man and had been away from my village for a long time, probably hunting. My main image from that time is of walking over the last hill before reaching home, and seeing the collection of small round huts clustered by the shore of a great lake. I was alone and returning with a great sense of triumph.

The land around was very green and the weather mild. Beyond the lake I could see mountains to the right and to the left a forest that would take uncountable days to cross, if it could be crossed at all. I could see no fields or obvious signs of cultivation; most of the land seemed to be forested.

My clothing was of animal hide but it was soft and supple, carefully stitched. I carried all that I needed for survival and valued each small possession in an almost mystical way. In my present life I tend to surround myself with clutter; the simplicity of my possessions in that earlier life gave me a great sense of freedom.

This snatch of time may have been pre-Celtic; the image is certainly a very ancient one. The Celts, who were farmers and weavers, arrived in Britain about 600 BC. The image I recall is of a far more primitive time, with apparently no woven cloth or land cultivation, although some land had been cleared of trees.

Farming actually began in Britain during the New Stone Age, around 3500 BC; stone-built villages are known to date from 2000 BC – one still exists in the Orkney Isles. The village I saw consisted of no more than a handful of round huts that I feel were built of wood with thatched roofs. This means that the time could have been as long ago as, say, 3000 BC, 1400 years before the building of Stonehenge. At this time houses were built of woven twigs plastered with mud, covered with a thatched roof. Corn growing had started, and it was harvested using sharp stone sickles.

I am uncertain about the country, but it was somewhere with a temperate climate which felt predominantly cool rather than warm. A settlement in Scotland during the late Stone Age would seem to be viable; some of the details certainly fit, and the landscape with its lakes and mountains is the closest that I have found to the region of that distant past.

Most important to me is that it was a moment of tremendous joy. This is the image that has come to me in dreams and at other times, whenever I feel a sense of achievement or fulfilment.

CHAPTER 4

Past Lives
Recovered

Hypnotic regression

My past-life memories are still present and occasionally a few more details arise, or I get a glimpse of another face superimposed on mine in the mirror, along with all the associated feelings of another time. These memories are now a mixture of several that I have always recalled – three in some detail, and six more that surfaced while I was undergoing a regression hypnosis experiment in 1988.

I originally underwent the experiment at the behest of a friend who was convinced that it would be worthwhile in my search for Mary Sutton's family. She introduced me to the hypnotist, Jim Alexander, who was already interested in investigating regression into past lives. My own need was to extract from the experiment whatever I could add to my memory of Mary's life in Ireland earlier this century. In particular, I hoped it would enable me to remember her surname, which had so far eluded me. As it happened, this wasn't necessary, but the experience did bring to light a number of extra details, and gave me an interesting insight into the method.

Hypnosis used in this way certainly helps to bring back long-forgotten material, and because it was Jim's experiment rather than mine we also explored other times and other lives together. This gave me the opportunity to remember more details about the lives I had always remembered without aid, and to look at several others I had not known about before.

The experience of hypnosis itself is curious. I had always been able to go into a light trance without realising that I was in fact hypnotising myself. What the hypnotist does is to guide a person into a state of self-hypnosis; having the hypnotist there in control makes it easier for the subject to focus, relax and go more deeply into the mind.

The hypnotist starts by taking the subject through a process of progressive relaxation, often by using some form of imagery such as visualising going down some stairs. This continues until the hypnotist can tell, by changes in the person's physical state and breathing patterns, that a deep enough trance has been reached.

After the first session, Jim was able to save the time and effort of 'talking me under' each time by using a trigger, in the form of a hand placed on my shoulder. This had the effect of putting me under almost instantaneously. In this state, I would have a vague awareness of my body growing limp and my breath slowing down; after that, all my attention would be on the images in my mind, with very little bodily awareness.

The sessions lasted about an hour each, though they never felt like more than five minutes or so. Once I was in trance Jim would ask me to see time moving, and I would see at a distance a series of unfocussed pictures. He would then ask me to go to a point in time that attracted me, or to a particular year or age. I would feel as if I were rushing forwards until I stopped, finding myself within a scene remembered either from this life or from a past one.

I have been asked whether this remembering is like watching a film; my experience is that it is more like remembering what you were doing a few weeks ago. I would feel an awareness of myself at that time and could look around me and describe what was there. I would also experience the emotions that the memory brought up, and the me sitting in the hypnotist's chair in real time would correspondingly cry or smile or shake with fear.

After looking at a particular point in time, Jim would ask me to go to another point; then, to test the consistency of what I had described previously, he might get me to dart back and forth between different points in different lives. Sometimes it felt like travelling in a roller-coaster across time as I sped backwards and forwards. Throughout, Jim would question me about what I was seeing and I would answer, at times hearing my voice in an almost disembodied way as if it were someone else's – the person I had been in the life I was recalling.

The depth of trance would increase throughout the session, reaching its deepest level towards the end. At the beginning, when the level of hypnosis was relatively shallow, the conscious me would be very aware of what was going on, which tended to interfere with the flow of answers. Towards the end, when the level of trance was much deeper, it occasionally became hard to speak, even though the detail I saw and felt might be quite fascinating. There seemed to be an ideal level during the middle part of a session when it was easiest to remember and talk about details and answer questions without conscious interference.

Frequently the details given under hypnosis are not as clear as those spontaneously recalled by children, which often makes these cases harder to verify. However, verification has been found for some cases of hypnotic regression, when the subject has come up with checkable information that he or she could not have come across in any other way.

One such case, described in *Reincarnation International* magazine (Issue 2, April 1994), is that of Ray Bryant who was regressed in 1980 by Joe Keeton, a hypnotist well known for his work in regression hypnosis. The evidence for this case was remarkable. Ray, a journalist on the *Reading Evening Post*, underwent hypnosis as part of an investigation for a series of articles. One of the personalities he described having been was Sergeant Reuben St—— (he was unsure of the surname) who had fought in the 47th Regiment of Foot in the Crimean War.

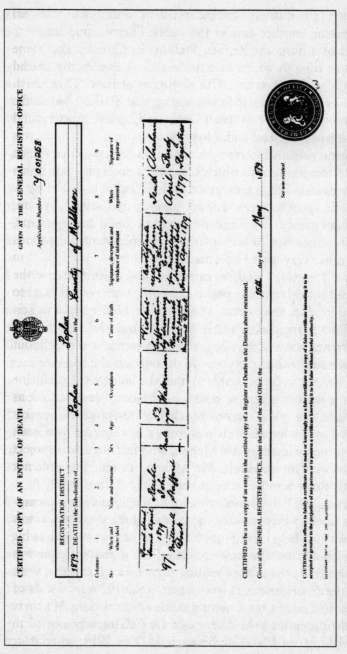

Under hypnosis, journalist Ray Bryant remembered a life as Reuben Stafford, a sergeant in the Crimean War. A death certificate confirming details remembered by Bryant was eventually traced.

51

Later, by chance, an independent enthusiast who was researching another case in the public library came across the record of a Sergeant Reuben Stafford in *Casualty Roll for the Crimean War*, by Frank and Andrea Cook, under the heading 'Assault on the Quarries, 47th Regiment of Foot'. Eventually a death certificate was also found, stating that Stafford had died by drowning in 1879 at Millwall Docks in London, exactly as Ray Bryant had described under hypnosis.

What especially interested me about the case was that it highlighted something with which I had had a problem – remembering surnames. The reason given by Joe Keeton is that in earlier centuries people were known almost exclusively by their Christian names. Even under hypnosis I found surnames difficult to remember. However, my own experiment did produce some other very useful information.

After *Yesterday's Children* came out I was quite excited when I received not only a strong positive response from readers, but confirmation of yet more details of Mary's life. Under hypnosis I had described a large house where Mary worked while still living at her parental home in the village of Portmarnock, near Dublin, and a doctor who visited the house in the only car she had ever seen. But I had not so far been able to trace the house or its occupants.

Some months after the book's publication I received a letter that gave me good reason to take seriously the memories I recalled under hypnosis. It was from a local garage owner who had been contacted by Mr Mahon, who had already helped me greatly with my research. Mr Mahon, an elderly resident of Swords Road who was a neighbour of the Sutton family in the 1920s and 30s, helped confirm some of the details of my memory of the family which assisted me in tracing the survivors. He felt that he could help identify the house, and so I sent him drawings of the front view and descriptions of the outbuildings and the lady owner. At the time of writing there is one house that seems to fit the description and was owned in the 1920s by a widow; I have yet to visit it for a more definite confirmation. My correspondent identified the doctor as a Dr Calahan who owned the Grand Hotel in Malahide between 1912 to 1919, when Mary

Sutton would have been between seventeen and twenty-four; he made a habit of visiting the local wealthy families, and would have visited the house I remember. My correspondent's father had been the doctor's valet.

I have always liked to back up my psychic experiences with solid evidence, and my search for Mary Sutton's family was a long piece of detective work. It was thrilling when at last I obtained objective confirmation of what I had always known. But it was not so easy to find verification of my other selves.

The lack of a surname has made it virtually impossible to trace a short life as a little boy, which I described several times under hypnosis. He was born in 1940 and died of some kind of fever in 1945 – I remembered the illness, though not the death. I gave his name as Charles S——, and I thought his father might have been called Raymond.

The road where he lived seemed to be Crest Hill or Hill Crest. I described a road sign with letters in the corner which looked like 'NW' and guessed that the location might be in north London, not far from where I was born in this life. I found there was a Hillcrest Avenue in the north-west London suburb of Hendon and drove there one day with the children. Although it didn't look quite right, I was at first quite excited to find that the Jewish family who had lived there at the right time had had a surname beginning with S and a son born during 1940. But on following this up I found that he was still alive.

There was very little to go on. My memories were of a self-contained, rather lonely child who spent most of the time on his own, either in the area in front of the house or in the garden, which had at least one mature tree and offered a view of the house suggesting late Victorian architecture. Indoors the family's time was mainly spent in the kitchen at the back, of which I was able to give quite a detailed description.

Almost opposite the house there was a side road going slightly uphill, but the route Charles most frequently travelled, holding his mother's hand, was downhill to a crossroads where I saw the road sign; it might therefore have belonged to an adjoining road. There was a game at the roadside, one foot on and one foot off the pavement, hopping up and down the herb; the road was virtually empty, with no danger from cars.

I put in quite a lot of work trying to trace Charles. With my mother I visited the Records Office in Hertford where the births, deaths and marriages for the whole country are kept on microfiche. Several trips and many hours' research took us up to the end of 1945 and revealed only one Charles S—— who was alive during the right period of years and died aged six in 1945. Charles turned out to be a very unusual name for children of the period; this was the only one we had found so far. However, he had lived in Gateshead in the north-east of England, and neither the name of the road nor that of his father matched.

In the end I had to give up the search. I had spent three or four days travelling to look through the records, which was a long and highly tedious task. My efforts to trace this rather sad and short life show how very hard it can be to substantiate even fairly recent memories.

The next life I recalled during my hypnosis sessions was the one before my Japanese life. I was a girl in a large family living in Southampton from about 1830, very close to the west docks. We lived on the east side of a small street lined with tiny, crowded cottages, which ran slightly downhill into the main quayside road. There I could see large ships; I described one very impressive ship with three tall masts, moored a little way off the loading jetty.

My father in this life was a violent drunkard; most of his aggression was directed towards our work-worn mother, who tried to keep us in food by taking in washing and mending. I had a friend, a tall, thin boy around my own age. We would try to get extra food by finding what we could at the docks, mainly scavenging goods that fell out of damaged packages; there was a sense of wrong-doing and a fear of getting caught, as though we might be accused of stealing. If we found anything I would take my share home for my mother, brothers and sisters.

I could remember hiding with a younger sister when my father returned home drunk one evening, and witnessing a beating; I realised that before long it would be my turn to be his scapegoat. It was after this incident that I seem to have made a decision to leave home. My sense of purpose echoed a recognisable personality trait that I carry in my present life – a stubborn determination to go ahead once a decision has been made.

It was a bad period in history to run away from home with nowhere to live. There was a risk of being arrested for vagrancy, so finding food and somewhere to sleep required caution as well as skill. It must have been spring because I can remember eating newly grown hawthorn shoots plucked from the hedgerows, while the nights were fairly cold.

My final memories were of lying near a horse whilst hiding in a stable, feeling weak and tired as well as hungry. I have the impression that this may have been only a few weeks after leaving home. I have no memory of the exact moment of dying; everything just seemed to merge – the smell and warmth of horses, the musty straw – into a strange, dissociated dizzy feeling in which I just drifted away.

One interesting detail in this past life is that the boy with whom I went on scavenging expeditions reminded me very much of my present-life husband, Steve. When people are regressed it is not at all unusual for them to discover that people involved in their current lives have also featured in previous ones.

It adds conviction to past-life stories when several related people are regressed independently and describe lives that were lived in the same time and place in which they were also in some way connected. One group of people who believe they have been drawn together over several lives was featured in the London Weekend Television series *Strange But True?* in 1994.

Their story began with the regression under hypnosis of Maureen Williamson in California. She recalled a life during the American Civil War as Becky, the wife of a man named John Daniel Ashford who was a wartime spy. During subsequent hypnosis sessions she began to identify people whom she knew in her current life as having lived alongside her in the same small town of Millboro, Virginia, in the 1860s, in former lives of their own. Eventually the hypnotist, Dr Marge Rieder, gathered no fewer than fifty people who were able under hypnosis to recall lives that were interconnected at this period. Each was able to give details that corroborated statements by the others, even without prior knowledge of what the others had said.

The most sceptical member of the group, and the most reluctant to undergo hypnosis, was Pat Greene, the man identified by Dr Rieder as having been John Daniel Ashford. Yet it was he who probably provided the most convincing evidence. A number of the group were taken to the now almost deserted town of Millboro, where they separately identified buildings and other details described in their accounts. Later, however, Pat Greene was shown an old photograph of the town and pointed out a house which, he said, had contained a room hidden underground. Some time later, a fire revealed that a hidden room did indeed exist under the house, unknown even to the owners.

There are several people I know now who seem to have played a part in my past lives. Curiously, too, in my glimpses of what I believe to be a future life in Nepal, at least one present-life friend seems to be with me. Over the years I have also met a number of people who have made a kind of instant emotional impact on me; sometimes the feeling has been one of relief, at other times a sudden fear of being parted again, and with yet other people there has been a sense of instant close rapport of the kind that usually takes years to develop. I have always accepted that these meetings have involved someone important from a previous life, even when I do not remember the life itself. As a child, my mother was the only person with whom I had a sense of long-term friendship.

Other people obviously have the same sense of instant recognition. One friend opened the subject by telling me that she had wondered for years if she would ever meet the person who she felt had been a sister in ancient Egypt. Although I couldn't remember having been there, I had to agree that the bond between us was strong. My friend told me of a courtyard with a fountain and a mosaic floor where the tiles created patterns of arcs and circles; the memory had been there from her early childhood.

In *The Children That Time Forgot* a little boy called Daniel said that some of his friends had been born at the same time as him. '... They all knew that they would meet up with each other while they lived on earth. When his mother asked him if he knew any of these friends, Daniel told her that he hadn't met them yet, but he was sure that as soon as he did meet one of them they would know each other straightaway.'

The accuracy of a past-life memory gained through hypnosis may not be 100 per cent perfect. It is liable to be similar to that of childhood memories, in that we may remember a particular event without being sure exactly how old we were, or which holiday we suffered an accident on, or the name of a school friend whose face we recall vividly; but it is the emotional content of our memories that affects us the most strongly.

This is why hypnotic regression can be useful as a form of therapy to help people come to terms with unresolved feelings which may have their origins way back in the past. Often traumatic past events – whether in this or previous lives – inhibit us from living a full life, although we do not remember the events themselves because of their painful associations.

Regression therapy is frequently successful in tracing the past causes of present-day stress. On occasion this necessitates looking not only at one's childhood but also at previous lives. Uncovering and confronting a long-buried trauma can release the emotional blocks around it, relieve the emotional pain, and enable one to see the present in perspective. Through the process of reviving and releasing the original memory, it is possible to let go of its emotional content.

In my own case, before embarking on hypnosis. I already knew about a number of past lives and the emotions associated with them. But hypnosis did help resolve my feelings in one instance, by enabling me to look more deeply into a memory that had been with me since childhood. I was aware that there was an important part of that memory that eluded me, as though it had been repressed.

The memories of this life were with me from a very early age; when I recalled them I felt inadequate, frustrated and very uncomfortable, yet they were insistent and I was unable to push them away. I knew that I had been a servant, possibly called Anna, in France during the first half of the eighteenth century. Before hypnosis I had mainly recalled the adolescent and young adult years, which were lightened by the company and friendship of another servant girl – who reminded me very much of a current friend. Most of our time seemed to be taken up with work; the only relief was in joking and giggling while we worked – and only when we knew there was nobody close enough to hear.

My household tasks were mainly confined to cleaning. I knew that I had started as a child by scrubbing floors and had then progressed to dusting and polishing the furniture, but I was considered clumsy and not to be trusted with any job that required skill. I very much disliked remembering Anna's sense of being stupid, immature and unattractive. In particular I was very aware of a lack of education, with accompanying feelings of inadequacy and worthlessness. When I first remembered this life I was not yet going to school and not bothered by the fact that I couldn't yet read. But remembering Anna's illiteracy would make me cringe with embarrassment.

I had always remembered this life begrudgingly, and the additional memory that was rekindled during regression took me by surprise. Under hypnosis I remembered the terrible day in 1716 when I was uprooted from a rural family home to become a skivvy in a town house in Boulogne. I was only seven.

The home I left had been a run-down farm worker's house; I could see the dirt paths around it, and old utensils leaning against the outside walls. My mother was a solidly built, pleasant woman and my father was a gentle, wiry-framed man who wore a constantly worried frown. I had a number of brothers and sisters who were raggedly dressed; we were obviously very poor, but despite this the atmosphere was comfortable and emotionally secure.

I recalled being taken by my father on a cart ride into the city;

he was quiet and looked very sombre. We arrived at a large house, and there he left me. I was taken to a small bare room high up in the attics; the walls were of slightly yellowing plaster and the only furniture was a wooden bed. At this point I was overcome with the sudden realisation that I would never see my family again. They did not want me: they had sold me into service. My grief and fear were overwhelming.

This was the episode of that life that I had been repressing. Once I had recovered this painful memory, even though the emotion was shattering, it enabled me to understand why remembering this particular past life made me feel so unloved and unwanted.

Hypnosis also cast light on the later part of Anna's life, which was spent moving from town to town trying to find casual work. It was hard to earn a living, and I became disturbed by the widespread squalor and poverty. As an adult my build took after that of my large, solid and fondly remembered mother, but where she had been maternal and lovable I always felt unloved and unlovable. There was no recollection of marriage or children, and as I grew older I seem to have become increasingly isolated emotionally. I remember only as far as about the age of fifty, and have no memory of Anna's death.

Considering this life afterwards, I was helped by being able to put it into its historical context. It was in the years running up to the French Revolution, when social conditions were very bad. I had always had a vague idea of the time Anna was living in, but had never before related it to the state of the country at the time. Now I could understand why I had been sold as a child: my parents had loved me, but had no other choice. I was able to come to terms with the hardship of my later life, and to release myself from the feeling that all the difficulties had somehow been my fault.

The life before Anna, again found under hypnosis, was difficult to remember. I was a young boy in 1650, and there was something wrong with me; I was aware of a space between myself and everyone else that suggested either deafness or autism. I couldn't talk or understand speech and, although I could see the workshop where my father cut timber, I did not understand enough to be of any help. It was a large open barn with chains and pulleys that were used to move large timbers. Judging by the size of the finished items, they were probably being prepared for building work. Several men worked here but my focus was mainly on my father, a very kind and tolerant man who looked after me and was the one person I knew I could trust.

Hypnosis enabled me to go even further back in time, as we jumped about between different periods. I had one very brief glimpse of a time as a small boy in a large Tudor house with floors covered in huge, cold stone slabs, and wall hangings that helped to cut out the draughts. There were small multiple panes of glass at the windows – unusual at that time, as glass was very expensive. I didn't see myself beyond the age of six, so I was unable to assess whether my role was that of servant or son of the house.

Even further back, on a date I gave as 1223, there was Gwen, the dumpy eighteen-year-old daughter of a family which, though not especially wealthy, was financially secure – they may have been traders. I was at a gathering to welcome home my brothers who had been away at the Crusades. (Later, I checked the date and found that it was consistent with the later Crusades.)

I saw a huge, solidly built wooden table on which was laid a variety of pies, bread, nuts and berries, suggesting an autumn feast. The house was of solid construction although it included a great deal of wood. Although my view was brief this felt like a good time – very secure, and simple but happy.

Before Gwen, I recalled having been Effan in Wales; asked what year it was, I said it was during the reign of Dafydd. I worked out afterwards that the year may have been around AD 800. At this time the great earthwork known as Offa's Dyke had been built to keep the Welsh tribes out of England, which had been colonised by the Saxons. There were a number of Davids who were leaders of the Welsh people.

As Effan I had a family of young children by the age of twenty. This life seemed very happy, despite problems typical of those days. Two of my children seem to have died of an illness which had struck the whole village, taking a number of children. This was probably a virus such as smallpox, to which the adults may have developed immunity.

I saw and described the village, a collection of rectangular buildings erected on wooden frames that were probably covered with wattle and daub (sticks and mud). None was very large. The weather was the main subject of interest on the day I was reliving; it had rained so heavily that the pathway out of the village was waterlogged and a cart had sunk into the mud so deeply that it seemed impossible to pull it out. There it remained, blocking the way, while the villagers tried to work out what to do about it. The cart was a simple flat bed made of wood, with solid wheels and drawn by oxen.

I was aware of my body as Effan: this time I was of a slight build and wore a dull-coloured, shapeless garment, woven of coarse wool thread. It was fairly scratchy but warm and long. I later found out that this weave was called homespun, and was consistent with the clothing of the time.

Although there are many theories about the mechanisms of reincarnation, my experiences have led me to draw my own conclusions. None of my past-life memories has put me in a prominent position, or even in particularly dramatic times. I missed the French Revolution by a few years and was a very young child during the Second World War. I never knew anyone famous. The most prestigious life was the one in Japan, the rest I spent often in poverty, and twice I was a very withdrawn little boy. Statistically speaking, this would seem fairly reasonable since the majority of people live ordinary, unremarkable lives. Six past lives as a girl or woman and four as a male would suggest a preference for being female.

Certain themes do seem to recur, including more than one instance of a violent father, and an ongoing sense of responsibility for failure and feelings of guilt for dying too soon. Above all, I am very much aware of being the same person throughout these lives; for me, the consistent feature is the development of the self through a series of changing circumstances. Change is essential for growth, and each life has its own set of challenges. Reincarnation is rather like going through a series of jobs in different cities; one remains the same person but gains more experience as different demands are made on one. Over the course of one life we slowly change and grow; over the course of many lives this process may continue. The spirit remains the same, released at death to rest between lives in another dimension.

CHAPTER 5

Between the Sky
and the Sea

Life between lives

If we continue after death, and can return to new lives over and over again, what happens to us in between? Where do we go? Although some people seem to come back quite quickly, most seem to spend a number of years somewhere else between each life. If there is a continuity, a linear connection linking the person who passes from one life to the next, there has to be somewhere for the energy of that person to go when it has left the physical form.

Many events over the years have prompted me to look further into this aspect of the soul's continuity. One of these was my daughter's experience following the death of my older brother. Michael died after a gliding accident in the summer of 1986, when Heather had just turned three. We had been unable to visit my brother or his family for a long time, so Heather hardly knew him. Then, within two weeks of Michael's death, Heather told me that she had had a strange dream that was 'not a dream', during which my 'magic brother' had visited her. I asked her why he was magic and she explained that he had been able to 'magic' himself into her room and had shown her a 'rainbow garden'.

As well as she could for a three-year-old, she told me about a garden that was not here but somewhere else, and that it was special. Though she lacked the necessary language, it was clear from her serious expression that she was trying hard to explain fully what had happened, and that she knew it was different from everyday life or ordinary dreams. She was a little confused by the experience and hesitant about talking about it, so I didn't press her to tell me more at the time.

I did tell Pat, my mother, about the incident; a week later we visited her, and by then Heather was happy to tell her grandmother about my magic brother who had taken her from her bedroom to see a rainbow garden. My mother had been away on a camping holiday and had seen a spectacular rainbow on the day of Michael's death – which of course caused her a lot of distress. She was very struck by the coincidence, and the idea of the rainbow became clearly fixed in her memory.

Pat showed Heather some photographs of both my brothers, and asked which one she had seen. Heather pointed instantly to Michael's picture, and said, 'That one! But he didn't have that hair' – meaning the moustache he had worn for a number of years. It was several weeks before my mother found out that Michael had shaved it off only a week or two before the accident.

Within a year Heather had forgotten about the incident, but the rest of us could not. Some years later I came across some accounts by people who had had near-death experiences (NDEs), which included descriptions of beautiful gardens and vivid rainbows, and I couldn't help but wonder about my daughter's description of a special garden and her certainty that my late brother had taken her there by magic.

Heather's story not only gave comfort to my mother and other members of the family; it also gave me courage. It was actually one of the catalysts that set me off on my search for my past-life children, because it helped me to accept the validity of my own experiences. By sharing something of the afterlife with my daughter, my brother had given me a sense of permission to forge ahead.

This was also healing for our relationship. Michael had been a padre in the RAF, and before that an Anglican vicar. In life not only did his views differ radically from mine but there was a communication gap between us, widened by his genius which created an intellectual gulf across which I could never reach. Yet it was Michael who brought us this vision – a vision of heaven, but one from which it was possible to return. For me this was compensation enough for the many things we had not been able to talk about or agree upon. It was as though he had found a way to tell me that we were *both* right.

When I underwent hypnosis to help with my past-life research, the period between lives was not explored at all. I was only asked to look at my previous lives, and Jim suggested that I see the periods in between as dark. My subconscious followed his suggestions – although I knew inside me that these periods were not dark, but full of light – and under hypnosis I only saw my lives. In view of the complexity of the emotions involved in my past-life research this was probably a necessary omission; I had quite enough to cope with at that time.

However, along with my memories of the life as Mary Sutton, I had always had memories not only of her dying but of the period after her death. I had always kept this to myself – even when writing *Yesterday's Children* – because I had felt nervous about sharing it with anyone. It seemed so far from everyone else's experience that I wasn't sure how people might react, and I had no way of proving that it had been real. At that point I had not come across anyone with similar recollections.

Dying as Mary was in fact the strongest image I had retained of that life, so although the remembrance was piercingly painful it was not difficult to summon up – it had haunted my dreams as a child. I remembered lying in a bed in what I now know to be the Rotunda Maternity Hospital in Dublin in the autumn of 1932. The room was brightly lit, probably with some of the earliest electric lighting in Ireland, which made the walls seem a very bright white in contrast with the dark cottage I remembered at home. As my illness had lasted for some time, I was kept in isolation and spent much of the time alone; the sense of loneliness added to my burden of grief at leaving my children behind. I was also alone at the point of death.

I knew that I had died. I could remember leaving the body, not just drifting out of it but being suddenly thrust out, rather like a buoy cut loose from its moorings. This, I later concluded, might have been due to the loss of the weight of the physical body, which no longer held me down.

After this sudden, swift upwards rush I was aware of settling some 10 feet above the body and slightly to one side of it. Although I was at a higher level than the ceiling, there was somehow nothing obscuring my view of the room. I remained there for some time, long enough to see Mary's husband come to the bedside, though how much later this was it is hard to say as my sense of time in this state seemed very vague, and certainly irrelevant.

What happened from this point on was no less clear. I was still looking back at my now vacant body when I seemed to be drawn from behind – almost sucked – into a long, narrow tube, like a fold in space, a dark vortex that wrapped around me and drew me into another dimension. Through it I travelled backwards, feeling somehow folded as though in a loose foetal position; slowly the hospital room drifted away from me, looking like a view seen through the wrong end of a telescope, and finally it faded completely.

Now, intensely bright beams of light began to emerge on either side of me. They were prismatic, like the shafts of a rainbow, but much, much brighter. To describe them as light seems somehow insufficient: the rainbow colours were much more vibrant than normal light, just as a real rainbow is much more vibrant than one drawn in crayons. The shafts of light passed by me at different angles and then spread out as though radiating from a central focus, though somewhat randomly.

I don't remember the actual moment when I emerged into a different place, but I know that I did emerge into somewhere very gentle and peaceful, far beyond any normal understanding of the words. This period is not clear in my memory, although it seems to be the stage remembered most clearly by other people who have had NDEs. This is the time at which they have usually found themselves meeting other people or going through a review of their lives. It seems possible, too, that it is from this stage that people occasionally return, in dreams or in spirit form, if they need to communicate with those whom they have left behind.

People who have NDEs are likely to remember this stage clearly because it is the one from which they return more or less directly. All I can remember of the time immediately after my arrival is that for a while there was a lot going on, some of which was perhaps to do with other people and some to my adjustment to my new state of being. What remains most clearly with me is the stage that followed this: it is still crystal-clear.

I found myself floating inside something like a soap bubble; above, below and all around me were other bubbles that I knew to be people. I was bodiless, and this didn't matter at all; there was no need for a body. The other bubbles seemed to have the peaceful energies of other people, also without bodies yet seeming complete, and I felt a total, peaceful empathy with them.

The sensation was of being almost like a single cell within a whole constellation of cells, yet also of being far too much of an individual entity to be contained in one unit so small. I was still aware of being myself, an individual soul. Every bubble glowed brightly with an energy that I took to be the basic life force that is ourselves, and they pulsated at rhythms which varied from a slow heart-rate beat to a steady vibration.

There was a great deal of background light all around, as though the whole life energy was expressed as light. It was difficult to see beyond it – it seemed to be reflected a little like the reflection of headlights in fog. Some of it took the form of strands like energy bands, mainly white through to blue in colour. But for their strange angles they could have looked like rivers. The overall feeling was of white light energy.

Enveloping everything was a feeling of calm, a unique calm in which nothing seemed to matter or hurt or worry. Here the existence I had left behind, physical life as we know it, seemed no more than a vague memory. Perhaps it simply became less important as time went by – though the notion of time itself had almost no meaning. There was no demarcation between day and night, just constant, peaceful light. Nor was there any sense of boredom. This is quite difficult, I find, for people to understand. This state of being is so utterly different from physical life that it is hard to put into words, but without bodies there is no need for activities and diversions. It is enough just to be. Yet, although apparently inactive, we seemed to end up as more than we were when we started.

The bubble-energies that were other people seemed to feel close all around me – yet this was nothing like being in a crowd of bodies, which can give rise to all kinds of feelings like hostility or claustrophobia. I had the sensation of being surrounded and enfolded by what I can only successfully describe as love. There was a wonderful sense of being incorporated within some much larger dimension of existence.

Although I had no doubt about the reality of this memory, it is probably not surprising that I had hesitated to speak of it to anyone. However, I gained confidence as I began to read about near-death experiences described by growing numbers of people who have been pronounced clinically dead for several minutes and have then returned to life. The more I found out, the more I recognised the similarities to my own memories of dying as Mary.

Most of these people have described an out-of-body experience that is instantaneous with the cessation of signs of life. It is common to see one's physical body below one, while the spiritual self that contains self-awareness is positioned above and often a little to one side of the body. Several people have been able to give accurate accounts of what was going on around them while they were clinically dead, and some have even described the activities going on in the next room. This adds considerable weight to the idea that, at death, the consciousness or spirit leaves the physical body but can still observe its surroundings. At this stage, there is usually a feeling of retaining an echo of one's physical shape.

Next, most people describe travelling down a tunnel, usually forwards, looking towards a light at the end. A number – often children – have described seeing rainbow-coloured light, and most talk about a bright white light. A feeling of absolute peace and wellbeing seems to be the most important part of the whole experience and the one most consistently referred to.

Sometimes a sense of light or peace occurs shortly before dying, and some people on the point of death have been known suddenly to become aware of a lost relative standing nearby, waiting for them. One of my patients once told me how she sat with her mother as she was dying. It was a dull, overcast day and her mother, who was terminally ill, had been listless and unresponsive for some time. Quite suddenly she looked past the daughter into a shadowy corner of the room and said, 'How beautiful. The sun is shining!' She died shortly afterwards, but her sense of upliftment and joy during her last moments helped her daughter to accept her death in a totally unlooked-for way.

After death, many people continue to see spiritual energies in human form; there are descriptions of the others there as people dressed in white and glowing with light. When I was surrounded by the bubble-energies, I was aware that they were people, and although they were non-physical they nevertheless seemed to have friendly expressions. I still find it hard to describe them without using words like 'face', 'expression' and 'people', even though, once beyond the tunnel, I cannot remember seeing any physical shape other than the simple, almost cellular energy-bubble.

It was not until I read *Transformed by the Light* by Dr Melvin Morse and Paul Perry that I discovered a description that was similar to my own experience of energy-bubbles. In this serious study of NDEs, the case study of 'Patient 44' recounts that she remembered having no body and being contained within 'some kind of essence' similar to the gelatine capsule used to contain medicines. The book also includes descriptions by others of being 'a ball of light' or of rolling into a ball when passing through the tunnel – which reminded me of my folded-up foetal position while in transit.

For me all this was a revelation. It was the first time that I had read an account that so completely backed up my own memories of the between-lives state. What Patient 44 had likened to a gelatine capsule and I had seen as being like a soap bubble was the most consistent state that I could remember between lives; to come across an experience identical to my own was extremely reassuring.

Dr Raymond Moody, author of another study of NDEs, *Life After Life*, found that of the many details given by people whom he questioned nine came up most frequently, and of these most people mentioned a few. They are: a sense of being dead; feelings of peace and painlessness; an out-of-body experience; travelling down a tunnel; seeing people of light; being greeted by a particular being of light; having a life review; a reluctance to return; and a personality transformation after returning to life.

My own memory of between lives incorporates the first five elements. This memory was of course a long-term one recalled from the time before my birth into this life, and is rather different from NDEs, which are usually brief and vivid. In my case I have no clear picture of meetings with other people or of the life review, during which people look back over their lives in order to evaluate their actions.

The life review usually occurs after first arriving in the other plane after death. Some people have described how they have experienced the events of their lives from the perspective of others, so that they have felt the pain that they themselves have inflicted. In becoming the victims of their own misdeeds they understand the hurt that may have resulted from their actions.

A vivid account of this kind of life review is given in *Saved by the Light* by Dannion Brinkley, who has survived two NDEs. He makes it clear that judging oneself is not something to be looked on lightly; experiencing the results of our own actions can be unimaginably punishing. While I have no memory of the life review itself, I do seem to have retained some consciousness of it in that I have been left with a very strong feeling that we are not judged by others but judge ourselves. This means that only we can change ourselves and take responsibility for our actions. And, ultimately, we have to forgive ourselves.

My memories of earlier deaths associated with other past lives are less distinct. With the Japanese life which ended in drowning, the tunnel seemed even more like a vortex; as the water seemed to move aside there appeared to be an anti-clockwise rotational movement of the tunnel, not unlike water going down a plughole except that it was moving upwards. On this occasion I travelled facing forwards and at the end of the tunnel I saw white light, sparkling with flashes of colour. In addition there seemed to be someone there to meet me at the end of the tunnel, but I remember no more than that.

When we have an experience that is not commonplace, any chance to compare our interpretation of it with others can be very comforting. In the summer of 1994 I was invited to take part in a conference on reincarnation and rebirth in Oslo, organised by the Norwegian psychologist and author Dr Rune Amundsen. I had never spoken in public before, so the experience was initially rather daunting, but it was well worth it.

One of the guest speakers was Dannion Brinkley. Having wrestled with words to try to describe the totally enveloping sense of peace and lack of negative emotions, the feeling of being a part of a larger energy and not isolated or alone, and the light and vibrancy of the between-life period, I was uplifted by Dannion's reassurance when we spoke afterwards. It was a great relief to me that someone with such a vivid memory of his own NDEs was able to identify with my own memory of the between-lives phase.

It was also reassuring at the same conference to receive positive input from conversations with a number of people who had similar memories to mine, such as the suddenness of moving out of body. Until that time I had felt very alone with my experiences.

Luckily I had always had access to some reference works that were relevant. One of the best known is the *Bardo Thodol*, known as *The Tibetan Book of the Dead*; this ancient text is designed to be read aloud to the dying and the newly dead to guide them through the afterlife, so that they can reach Nirvana without having to be reincarnated. The description of the first state arrived at is very similar to the modern NDE accounts, including brilliant light and feelings of extreme peace. Mentioned later are out-of-body experiences and a halo of rainbow light, also common in NDEs.

But there was one description, occurring quite a long way into the text, that I instantly recognised because it was so similar to my main memory of the between-lives state. This is called the 'Central Realm of the Densely Packed', where one merges into the halo of rainbow light in which one obtains Buddahood.

This reminded me very much of the feelings I recalled of being bathed in light, and surrounded on all sides with an apparently infinite number of other light-emitting energies, closely packed together and resonating with each other. Curiously, though, there seems to be an anomaly here, since this is the state leading to Nirvana, from which one need not return to be reincarnated, and to which I should therefore not have been able to aspire.

Much of the text is addressed to the dying or dead who are afraid to join the light or are nagged by doubts; these fears are described in terms reminiscent of descriptions of hell and demons. I have no memory of having any such fears. It is possible that this condition is analogous with nightmares; there is the suggestion that it is of the sufferer's own making, which corresponds with my own feeling that we are our own judges and punish ourselves. It seems likely that fears and guilts and regrets at the moment of death could impede complete acceptance of the light, and could indeed continue to affect one in future lives.

In my researches, I also came across one account of the between-lives phase by someone with whom I feel great empathy. As well as remembering and tracing her previous-life circumstances, some years later Shanti Devi described what she remembered from between her lives. She told of darkness just before her death, followed by a dazzling light and being out of her body in a vaporous form. She saw four men in very bright saffron robes (the attire of Hindu priests) who took her up to a garden that was beautiful beyond description. Here she experienced herself as very small, 'the size of a thumb'. There was no day or night – all was full of light. I was particularly fascinated by her recollection of feeling tiny in size, which I too had felt.

For many years I wondered about the idea of our entire life energy being contained in something so very small. Although this was how I had remembered it, it is quite a difficult concept to grasp in this life. Of course, each one of us starts this life as a single cell, which divides and grows into a foetus and then into a baby, so it is true that even without the premise of reincarnation we all start our lives as microscopic beings.

Nevertheless, I was still wrestling with the idea when science came to the rescue. I was reading about the 'Big Bang' theory, the point of conception of the universe as we know it, when the whole universe, all matter and all energy, was originally contained in something as small as a single atom. To think of everything, all of the stars and galaxies, all matter and energy, compressed into such a tiny mass is almost beyond imagination. But if we can accept that, it is not only easy but entirely logical to think of our own individual energies existing within tiny units.

The sense of the energy between life as inclusive, that as single entities we are not alone but a part of something larger, is not necessarily confined to the between-life state. It has been experienced by mystics of all religions, and also by people going about their ordinary lives, as I did when I was in my early teens.

One very still and mild evening in the late summer of 1969 I was walking home from a friend's house. As I passed the remains of the defensive ditch built outside St Albans in Roman times there was little traffic along the road. A light breeze rustled the leaves of the many trees which overhung the pavement. My brisk, steady pace took me in and out of the long shadows in an almost hypnotic rhythm, and my awareness was drawn to the trees, to their energy and the life within them.

Then, quite rapidly, a most peculiar thing happened. Had I ever heard of the term, I might have described it as an out-of-body experience. But I was not just out of my body: I was *within* something else. Perhaps because I was preoccupied with the trees it was as if some part of me, some energy, had become joined with the energy of the trees. It didn't stop there; that part of me began to be stretched out, to join with other living things, at first with plants, then further afield until I seemed to be touching a tremendous variety of life forms, both plant and animal.

Within the brief moments of this inexplicable experience I sensed an awareness of life as a whole unit, of everything joined together, of a connection between every single aspect of living energy. I was also aware of the way in which everything was constantly changing form as each being lived and died, always returning to the energy of the whole. I understood life and death as a constant cycle, and that individuals are never completely separate from the whole. I experienced my whole lifetime as though it were a single picture, and realised the sense of continuity, of lives after lives. I understood that there was no need for fear, no need to feel alone. At the same time I felt insignificant but not without value, for I was integral with that energy which was the whole of life.

This realisation left me both comforted and exhilarated. It was as though all the things that I worried about were no longer important. No longer did I feel like a separate individual; I knew that I was a small part of something much greater, within which we were all connected, in very much the same way as the individual bubble-energies were connected in the between-life time that I remembered. Yet, although I felt that I understood what had happened, it raised many questions for me. Afterwards, I tried to assess the event and to understand its essence in a logical way.

Because I had past-life memories the notion that we continue was not new to me; but at this point, at the age of sixteen, I had never considered life as a single unit of energy, and I wondered about this experience of wholeness. In fact for many years I read and studied whatever I could that related to this concept.

My reading included the psychology of Carl Jung, who created the term 'collective unconscious'; this, I felt, was a good way of seeing how we are connected with the energy of which we

74

are a part, through sharing a deeper part of our mind and life energy. Later I came across the theory of Gaia, first put forward by the distinguished British chemist James Lovelock and named after the earth goddess of classical mythology. This theory describes the world as a living, self-regulating unit of which we are a small and possibly dispensable part; it states that the balance of nature does not come about by chance but is positively regulated, and within it all living things on this earth are connected and interdependent.

CHAPTER 6

Choosing to Return

Decisions in rebirth

The hypnosis experiment suggested that the shortest time that I had spent between lives was eight years, but from the evidence gathered during research this may not represent an average. Some of the children who remember previous lives have had a very short return time – a few inside a year. It seems clear from their accounts that very often those who return promptly with vivid past-life memories are driven by a sense of unfinished business. But this does not, apparently, apply to everyone. What makes us choose to come back at certain times, and under particular circumstances?

The impression I have retained from my memories of the between-life state is that sooner or later the spiritual self feels an urge to return, a kind of wanting to be. It seems likely that this need to re-experience life in a physical form is prompted by the need to do or to learn something in order to feel complete and fulfilled.

From my own past-life experiences, as well as the many studies of the subject, it is clear that throughout many lifetimes we are born into a variety of different circumstances and nationalities.

How much choice do we actually have? Is it true that we are born into difficult lives in order to pay off karmic debts? What other factors might play a part in our choices – if we have a choice? Is there a reason for returning to a particular place?

I would never wish to devalue anyone else's beliefs, but my own experience and gut-feelings do not always correspond with some of the traditional teachings or current New Age thinking. For example, I do not believe that we choose our parents or our next birthplace in any conscious or thinking sense. Nor do I feel that we are reborn into difficult circumstances as a punishment for past misdeeds. I feel that the hardship or otherwise of the lives we choose is almost incidental. Factors like race, wealth and social circumstances exist in the physical state; in the between-life state they are totally irrelevant. It seems that our return from that state is much more like being drawn towards certain circumstances as though by the winds and tides of subconscious instinct – just as we are drawn to friendships in ways that are subtle and reflective rather than reasoned and calculating.

I was interested to come across a description of the Japanese between-lives state, called *gusho*, which tallies with many of my own conclusions. The belief is that the spirit returns to become a similar individual within seven generations. The spirit is clearly differentiated from the mind and body: it is the spirit that is reincarnated, while the mind and body are inherited from the parents.

The physical aspects of the next life are unlikely to affect the choice of life, because they are not relevant to the spirit. These would include such factors as race, physical size, ability and strength, which to the spirit would be incidental. Some theories on reincarnation teach that to be born with a physical or mental disability is either the result of misdeeds in a previous life or chosen by the soul in order for us to learn a particular lesson. I myself believe that the explanation is much simpler; that disabilities are neither inflicted nor chosen, but come about purely through physical or genetic accidents.

The mind is more closely linked to the spirit than is the body, but while the ability to make good use of one's intelligence probably depends on the personality, the intelligence itself is likely to be an inherited factor. What seems most consistently to continue from one life to the next is the personality, which is the expression of the spirit, and which needs to acquire new experiences in order to learn and to grow.

Changing lives from one to the next might be likened to changing one's clothes, in that the outward appearance alters but the person on the inside remains the same. Each time we may move on and grow into a new environment, developing different facets of the same basic personality. With altering surroundings and circumstances the demands made on us vary, giving us the chance of a multitude of possible experiences and the opportunity to learn about each other and ourselves.

If we choose a particular emphasis in one particular life, it may be in order to balance aspects of the personality that are slightly out of kilter. In my current life, for instance, I have found myself – like many women today – in circumstances which have ultimately led me to give up the role of 'victim', in which my early childhood placed me, in order to become more myself. Another person might be imbalanced in a different way, perhaps needing to learn to be less aggressive or arrogant. If we are at all alert, it is not difficult to learn from those around us in this life what we need to develop as well-rounded, harmonious individuals.

I believe that the most important factor drawing us into any particular life is our empathy with other people, often those with whom we have shared experiences in past lives. It has been shown under experimental conditions that we are drawn to people who are similar in outlook and family background, even before a word is spoken. This has been demonstrated by an experiment called the Family Systems Exercise which is used to train family therapists, and is described in *Families and How to Survive Them* by Robin Skinner and John Cleese. The members of a group of people who had not met before were each asked to choose, without exchanging any words, others from the group whom they felt would fit into their family. When they finally sat down to discuss what they had in common, it was found that they shared values, attitudes and even life experiences.

Particularly intriguing were the four who were the last to choose each other – and therefore might be thought of as the left-over people, and perhaps less liable to have anything in common. They found that they had all been adopted, fostered or brought up in children's homes. The concept is fascinating. It is clear that we are unconsciously drawn to the people who are most like us or, more to the point, think most like us. This explains why certain people tend to band together in like groups. Without having to exchange a word we seem to have an instinctive empathy with others who have passed through the same kind of experiences as ourselves.

This made me wonder whether the same sort of instinctive awareness could be in some way responsible for helping us find a life in which we will fit. Most people – though certainly not all – tend to fit in with their own families. Much of this can be explained by the fact that we share inherited factors, and that we grow up learning the rules and preferences of our families. But is the empathy between family members due purely to shared genes and environment? Have we also shared experiences that we may not remember, but to which we instinctively respond? Sometimes we feel closer to friends than to family members. In my case, I feel very comfortable with the members of my past-life family, Mary's children, entirely without the benefit of any blood relationship in this life.

There is evidence to suggest that groups of people remain attached to each other as a unit, drawn back to be together again over a number of lifetimes. Frequently people claim to have met friends or to have been married to their partner in one or several previous lives, suggesting a commitment spanning generations. Indeed, there have been whole families who claim to have existed together as families in previous lives.

Brian L. Weiss MD is an American psychiatrist who runs workshops on regression. In his book *Through Time into Healing* he describes how on a number of occasions members of the same family have attended his workshops together, to discover afterwards that they have unknowingly regressed to the same past-life area and time when they were also related – though not necessarily in the same relationship. One such family was featured in the *Oprah Winfrey Show* in 1993. The members had undergone regression hypnosis separately, and all had independently described their roles as different members of the same previous-life family.

The exchange or reversing of roles is interesting. In this life we reverse roles when we grow from being children with parents into parents with children. Just as we understand our own parents better when we have children, we may learn something of the role of another by being in their place next time. As a child, I frequently felt that my relationship with my mother should be different. I felt that in the past I had been the older person and responsible for her.

My mother had an attitude to parenthood that is not only relevant in this respect, but also sums up the change in relationships that we may experience across time. She has always said that a child is not yours, since you can't own people; having a child is more like a loan. You should treat children with fairness, respect their opinions and encourage them to do the same for others. With luck you may then find that you can be good friends when they become adults. If our roles change around it is easy to see why a mother or daughter may feel more like a sister, and why some friends feel like family members. The one consistent feature of these relationships is that of supportive friendship.

I also feel that children's so-called 'imaginary friends' may hark back to friendships from other lifetimes. According to a recent study, 'imaginary friends' fall into two distinct types. In the first, the 'friends' are clearly pure fantasy, invented in play. But there is a second type in which the friend is a realistic person whose characteristics remain constant and unembellished by the child describing them. One girl described her friend as the old man who used to live in her house; he sat by the fire in a big chair and smoked a pipe. A boy described a man who looked like an older version of himself, and was able to answer some of his questions. In the case of my own imaginary friends there certainly seemed to be some long-term connection, though it was not one that I could specifically identify.

We may well be drawn back repeatedly to those with whom we had previously found empathy or experienced interaction. This doesn't mean that every life will be good and surrounded by old friends, but that there should be a chance to be with some of the people who have been important before.

Of course, there are people who find that they have no real connection with their families, or indeed have very difficult or damaging relationships, or other serious difficulties. It is easy to put challenging circumstances down to 'karma', and to say that someone who suffers from the actions of others is therefore responsible for their difficulties. This is quite a harsh judgement, and I think the situation is considerably more complex than that.

For one thing, while we may come into life determined to sort out a particular type of situation or relationship, other people in our lives have entered existence with their own agendas, for which we are not responsible. I very much agree with the comments of Dr Brian Weiss in *Through Time into Healing* when he described a case in which hypnotherapy was used to help the healing of a woman who had been sexually abused as a child.

People often bring up the idea of 'Karma': that as far as life-time experiences and circumstances go, what we sow in one life-time is what we reap in the next. This is not always strictly true. I believe that experiences like these are not necessarily punishments from the past, or even lessons or patterns carried forward from past lives. By choosing to come into a particular family or constellation of circumstances you have not agreed to submit to abuse. However, you have agreed to participate in a certain lesson or type of drama. You still have free will about how a particular lesson or teaching is carried out and so do the other individuals who have chosen to share the lifetime with you. Just because you have agreed to play a role in this family, abuse is not the invariable result. Part of the learning process is learning not to choose the more harmful or destructive paths.

Growth can occur easily and joyfully as well as through struggle, and there are many gradations between the two.

The key here is that other individuals around you also have free will, and you may suffer the effects of their actions through no fault of your own. In times of war and other national crises, for example, all kinds of individual and social factors come into play; individual victims may have done nothing to 'deserve' their misfortunes, though they may well find opportunities for developing characteristics like courage and tolerance. On a more individual basis, although you may have a need to work out past experiences with a particular person, you may not necessarily be able to develop a good relationship with them and should not consider yourself a failure if you don't succeed. It may even be necessary to your development to move away from them. In the end, in order to relate properly with others, what we need primarily is to understand ourselves.

While I do not believe that we choose certain circumstances as a punishment, my own experience suggests that many of us feel a need for forgiveness, and particularly for self-forgiveness. This may be another important factor in drawing us to particular life circumstances.

Indeed, the issue of forgiveness often draws the spirit back shortly after death. Probably a number of people have had similar experiences to that of my friend Mrs Kemp. A very down-to-earth lady living in south Northamptonshire, Mrs Kemp is not usually given to psychic visions. Yet she told me how she had had a visit from her late father. He had died very suddenly at a time when she had not seen him for six or seven weeks, and her sadness at losing him was compounded by a sense of guilt.

About six months after his death she woke up one night to see him sitting in a chair across the room; he was quite solid and not at all ghost-like. She insists that she was awake and did not feel afraid. He was sitting slightly forward on the chair in a characteristic attitude, wearing his glasses perched on the end of his nose. (Her mother later said he had been buried in his glasses.) He looked at her and smiled gently. From that moment she felt calm and relaxed, freed of all her concern, her feelings of bereavement, and above all her sense of guilt.

The need to feel forgiven can be very powerful. Among the psychic experiences of my teenage years there was one that stood out because of its difference from the others. For me, it was not altogether pleasant. For several evenings running, as I was reading in bed, I saw quite clearly a man who I knew had died at least a year earlier. He was not a person I would have chosen to see, since I had good reason to distrust and dislike him.

The first time he appeared, I simply felt aware that there was someone next to me; I looked up to see him standing there, looking uncomfortable and embarrassed. Then he spoke to me, and asked me to forgive him for his past behaviour. I was a little shocked and tried to tell myself this wasn't happening. At first I ignored him but, to my discomfort, he reappeared on several successive evenings.

I finally realised that he would keep coming back until I accepted his presence and gave him an answer. So in the end I did acknowledge him, but I told him I still felt that the way he had behaved was wrong. Forgiveness, I believe, comes with the ability to understand and let go of the painful past; at that point the effects of his behaviour were too close to me for me to be able truthfully to forgive him. Even though I could not give him the answer that he seemed to want, it may have been the one he expected; apparently it was enough, because after that he left and never returned.

The one thing that grew out of this for me, as from other events, was that we all have a need for forgiveness. The negative emotions that we carry around with us, either through one life or from one life to the next, are destructive both to ourselves and to others. The need to let go of or come to terms with them may be a strong element in our choice of next life.

Above all, as I experienced in my between-life state, there is a need for self-forgiveness. We are not, ultimately, judged or punished by others, but do so ourselves – although our feelings of guilt may attract the judgement of others. I am not suggesting that we should not feel guilty if we do harm, but many people carry around an unnecessary sense of guilt and unworthiness. Setting down this burden liberates us to live more fully and creatively.

I entered my present life with a strong sense of guilt at having deserted a family of young children, which drove me to trace the life of Mary Sutton. Even after discovering my lost family, I had yet another challenge from the past to face. In April 1994 I was recording an item with ABC News *20/20* for the American publicity for *Yesterday's Children*. I found myself in the Rotunda Maternity Hospital in Dublin looking for the room where I had died as Mary, ill and in great pain from pneumonia, gas gangrene and toxaemia.

I knew that the room was on the corner of the building and one floor up. Although I had not been near the hospital in this present life, I was able to sketch the location of the room with some confidence and sent this to the producer, Rob Wallace, a week or so prior to the trip. From this the hospital matron was

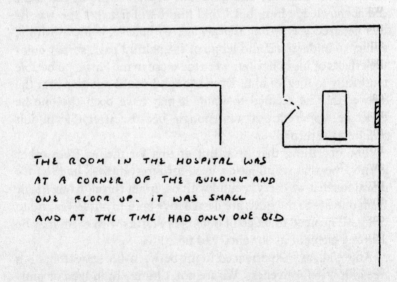

THE ROOM IN THE HOSPITAL WAS
AT A CORNER OF THE BUILDING AND
ONE FLOOR UP. IT WAS SMALL
AND AT THE TIME HAD ONLY ONE BED

My sketch of the location of the room in the Rotunda Maternity Hospital in which I remembered Mary dying.

able to locate the only room which fitted my description. It was a small isolation room and was indeed at a corner of the building and one floor up.

When I entered the room I immediately began to feel very uncomfortable. I was increasingly certain that it was the right room, although I was confused at first because it had two windows and I only remembered one. However, when I placed myself behind the door where the bed had been, and lowered my head to pillow height, I realised that from that angle I could only see one window.

In that room I became more and more ill at ease. I went through a short interview, but then my feelings of panic and anguish became too much to bear; I had to excuse myself and backed out of the room. Much later the significance of this style of exit sank home – that was how I had remembered leaving last time, leaving the dying body of Mary and going backwards through the tunnel.

Once outside, I felt a need to be certain about the details; I had remembered seeing people passing by the door, but there was now a partition in the way blocking the view. Luckily the matron was able to tell me that this had been built in the 1960s and had definitely not been there in the 1930s when Mary was a patient.

The next day, returning for further filming, I found it a little easier to enter the room, and after a while it became less traumatic, presumably as I was able to let go of this one pervading memory – the anguish of Mary's death. I did not forget it, but now I was able to let it heal. I wasn't sure if the film crew were aware how far they had been instrumental in this healing process, but I was grateful that they had persuaded me to find the room. Even though it was weeks before I felt completely at ease again, the experience gave me a unique opportunity to gauge the importance of facing and releasing the past.

At last I was able to let go of the sense of guilt at dying, and accepted that when battling against so many physical odds it was not a sin to have given up the fight to live. I finally forgave myself completely for deserting the children through what was, after all, an inescapable death. And by letting go of the past I resolved another cause of pain, making room for a little more peace of spirit.

If my past-life memories are typical, as seems likely, one thing that is clear is that nobody is better than anyone else and that none of us is really in a position to judge others. We have probably all been born into poor, ordinary backgrounds and into a variety of nationalities and races.

Some natural variations such as homosexuality are seen by some as a mistake – and by some as a sin – although there is an obvious advantage for an over-populated society to include productive and useful people who do not add to the population figures. I do not subscribe to the theory held by some people that homosexuality is the result of having been a different sex in one's past life. Dr Satwant Pasricha has noted that there is no such connection among those children who remember being of a different gender in their previous life.

Variety is essential for survival. In nature, variety ensures the survival of species. If we were too similar physically we would be susceptible to the same illnesses, so we have different blood groups and skin types, ensuring that, when new or old diseases break out, there will always be some survivors. Psychological variety is also necessary for our survival. The rich achievements of humanity over the centuries have depended on the existence of both creative, emotional people and steady methodical types; on ordinary intelligence as well as genius.

We all live under the shadow of our many and various pasts. They are an integral part of us and can help or hinder us, depending on how we draw on our deeper feelings. One of the purposes of our different lives is to learn to interact with others, and we are presented with a variety of ways of doing so. Certainly we can and should learn from our past and understand our relationships with others in the context of previous experience. And since the demarcation of our roles is only temporary, the only real relationship that counts is one of equality, caring, love and respect. Perhaps this is what we

really come back to learn: to heal our relationships with ourselves and others so that we can express in our physical lives
the oneness from which we all come and to which we return
between lives.

CHAPTER 7

Precognition

Visions of the future

My purpose in writing this book is to share my sense of the continuity of life through many lifetimes, both past and future. Before going on to describe what I have seen of my future lives, it may be useful to look at the whole subject of precognition. It is a human ability as old as time. Texts from all the ancient civilisations contain descriptions of dreams and prophecies, which were taken seriously and acted upon. Today it is an area that is still surrounded by scepticism and misunderstanding. Yet I believe that the ability to see or sense the future may in fact be an innate human faculty which could be cultivated, even if we do not yet understand fully how it works, and it may be far more widespread than modern Western society seems able to accept.

Precognition, which literally means foreknowledge, can take many forms, from the most subtle feeling of *déja vu* right through to a powerful vision of some event many years hence. It can come in dreams or while we are awake; it can happen unexpectedly or as a result of concentrated meditation. It may manifest simply as a vague feeling of knowing what is going to happen next; most people have experienced thinking of a friend just before that friend telephones. Or it can take the form of a premonition (forewarning), for example a feeling that it would not be a good idea to travel on a particular day. What classifies these experiences as precognition is that the event foreseen actually occurs.

Probably we all need to discuss such experiences more. Many adults are still inhibited about talking about them, though children are less affected by preconceptions about the world and generally find it easier to accept the evidence of their own senses. Early in my own life it seemed quite ordinary to wait for things to happen once I had 'seen' them – and they did happen. Even so, there would be occasions when the accuracy of my precognition would take me by surprise. In those days I learned to keep quiet about my foresights; nowadays people are becoming more open-minded, and it has become increasingly apparent to me that most people have had certain experiences that they would like to be able to talk about. I am quite certain that it is not unusual to have premonitions or premonitory dreams, as well as a variety of other so-called paranormal experiences.

If precognition is a natural human gift, what is its purpose? Nature usually endows us with abilities that are of some use to our survival, as individuals or as a group. If some special skill improves the chances of survival, in humans or animals, it tends to be passed on to future generations. In a group of animals only a small number is needed to raise the alarm when they sense forthcoming danger, and the whole group is alerted into action.

Perhaps every species has developed some precognitive ability, which in the human race may be enhanced in a small percentage of individuals, or may reside in a less accessible part of the brain so that only a few are consciously aware of it. What cannot be denied is that it does exist, and should therefore be regarded in the same way as any other skill – as a natural faculty. And its purpose, at least in part, could be to warn us of impending danger or disaster.

A good example is given by Richard Lazarus in *Beyond the*

Impossible. An American parapsychologist, Professor William Cox, believes that many people act on premonitions in everyday life although they are quite unaware of it. Over a six-year period he took statistical details of the numbers of passengers who usually travelled by rail; he found that, on days when accidents occurred, far fewer passengers than usual were on board the trains involved. Using a computer, he calculated that the statistical odds against there being fewer passengers on those days by chance were over a million to one. In other words, a proportion of potential travellers had some unconscious knowledge of the future and acted on it, without consciously realising they were doing so.

Many premonitions and clairvoyant visions involve warnings of floods and other natural disasters. When such predictions come true, they are treated as curiosities. But it may be that, even if we can't prevent the disasters from happening, taking note of the forewarning could help us to stave off some of their worst effects.

The prophecies of the sixteenth-century seer Nostradamus are still popular reading today, particularly as we approach the millennium, traditionally a time when major change is expected. *Nostradamus: The Next Fifty Years*, a new translation and explanation of his prophecies by Peter Lemesurier, includes many forecasts attributed to our near future. One of these is of flooding throughout most of Europe, notably in Greece and Italy and including Britain. This all became more pertinent in the light of the devastating floods in northern Italy during November 1994.

Nostradamus is not the only person to have spoken of widespread flooding as an increasing, ongoing problem for a number of years in our present times. Our recently acquired knowledge about the effects of global warming may now render psychic predictions unnecessary, but a number of people were predicting flooding long before there was any indication of global warming. One of these was a dowser whom I met many years ago; for years he had had a recurrent dream of standing on high ground looking out over a flooded landscape, knowing that many of the lower-lying areas of Britain were under water. Dowsing is the art of finding water using a natural instinct. This is either felt through one's outstretched open hands or enhanced by holding dowsing rods or a forked twig. Everyone can dowse, but some people have a particular gift and are able to determine depth and flow, and are often able to find things other than just water, like metals or minerals.

I, too, have had visions of future flooding. In the autumn of 1989 a women's magazine asked readers for accounts of their experiences of precognition. Assuming that their interest was serious, I wrote to them suggesting that it might be of greater value if people were to write in with their premonitions before the events foreseen occurred, so that the phenomenon could be put to the test.

Having recently had a premonitory dream which for once was not purely personal, I felt I had a useful contribution to make. I told them I had seen the River Severn breaking its banks and causing major and life-threatening floods, the worst in that area for many years, and that this would happen in about four months from the date of my letter. (Four months is the usual time lapse between my premonitory dreams and the actual event.) I also told my family and friends about the dream.

Some four months later, in February 1990, there was indeed terrible flooding when the River Severn broke its banks; numbers of people were cut off and had to be rescued. There had been little warning and the floodwater covered large areas, threatening towns and farmland alike. Encouraged by the friends with whom I had shared my dream, I wrote again to the magazine asking if they had filed the original letter as requested. I never had a reply. Annoyed at this lost opportunity for proper documentation, I then wrote a brief letter to the *Mail on Sunday* about the incident; at least they thought it worth printing.

Another of my dreams about flooding was more confusing, as there seemed to be water everywhere and I couldn't pinpoint the region at all. A few months later, in January 1994, the dream made more sense when there were floods all over Europe and Britain.

Other disasters have been predicted in this century; in some

Flood warning

IN the autumn, when a woman's magazine was taking a look at premonition, I wrote to say that I'd had a dream about the River Severn breaking its banks and threatening lives through flooding. I forecast that this would happen in about four months' time.

Perhaps it would have been more useful if I had written to the river authorities.

JENNY COCKELL,
Wood Bureote, Northants.

From The Mail on Sunday, *18 February 1990.*

cases, taking them seriously might have mitigated some of the effects. With others, as so often with predictions, it had been harder to pinpoint time and place beforehand. To take an example, in the 1960s an American psychic, a hairdresser called Joseph Delouise, described a number of his prophetic dreams on television. In November 1967 he predicted the collapse of a bridge; three weeks later the Silver Bridge across the Ohio River collapsed, killing forty-six people. Early in 1968 he foresaw major riots in Chicago that spring; on 7 April there was such severe rioting in the city that the governor had to deploy five thousand Federal troops to restore order.

In May 1969 Delouise also went on record on American television predicting an air disaster that would kill seventy-nine people before the end of the year; the number 330 was in some way connected with the event. On 9 September at 3.30 a DC-9 was in a mid-air collision with a light aircraft near Indianapolis. Including the pilot of the smaller plane, the death total was seventy-nine.

Occasionally detailed and dramatic predictions have been used in fiction by writers who were unaware that they were foreseeing real events rather than drawing on a vivid imagination. The spiritualist W. T. Stead, for instance, wrote in 1886 a short story recounting a tragedy very similar to the sinking of the *Titanic*; ironically, he was to be one of the 1513 passengers who died on the doomed vessel. But it was the novelist Morgan Robertson in 1898 who came closest to describing the disaster in detail, including a description of a ship nearly identical to the *Titanic*. His fictional ship was about the same size and speed, with a carrying capacity of 3000 people, and he called it the *Titan*. This 'unsinkable' vessel, like the *Titanic*, sailed on her maiden voyage from Southampton on a luxury trip to America, and sank in April in the same part of the Atlantic after hitting an iceberg, with heavy loss of life. Robertson's book, called *Futility*, was published fourteen years before the *Titanic* sank in April 1912.

There are records of other tragedies forecast before the event. The day before President John Kennedy's assassination, a woman telephoned the White House to say that she had a dream that Kennedy would be killed in Dallas. She was not the only one to have made such a prediction. In 1956 a medium, Mrs Jeanne Dixon, predicted that 'a blue-eyed Democrat' would become President in 1960, and would later be assassinated. On the day of the assassination she told her dinner guests, 'Something dreadful will happen to the President today.' She also predicted the deaths of President Roosevelt in

1945, Mahatma Gandhi in 1948 and Winston Churchill in 1965.

Foreseeing one's own demise may seem a little odd, but it happens quite often. During the weeks before his fatal road accident the actor James Dean is reported to have told friends of a terrifying recurring dream in which he was in a crash. Abraham Lincoln dreamed of seeing a coffin guarded by soldiers and surrounded by mourners; when he asked who was dead he was told that it was the President, who had been killed by an assassin. He told this dream to a close friend, Ward Hill Lamon, who wrote an account of it five days before Lincoln's assassination at Ford's Theatre in Washington.

These experiences are not confined to public figures. Mrs Saunders, by then an elderly lady, told me about her son while we sat in her bungalow in a small village near Banbury in Oxfordshire. All his life he had told his family, much to their concern, that he would not reach twenty-one, and he refused to make any career plans. This didn't seem to stop him enjoying life, and he was known for his easy-going disposition. A few weeks before his twenty-first birthday he was mending a tractor when the support timber broke, causing the machine to fall and crush him. He died instantly. One can only hope that his foreknowledge helped his parents to cope with the tragedy that fate seems to have planned for him so far in advance.

A number of my friends and acquaintances have had premonitions. As a result of the publicity for *Yesterday's Children* I was contacted by a portrait photographer, Harold Fountain, for whom I had modelled as a child and teenager and whom I had not seen for some twenty years. He told me that he had dreamed of Windsor Castle going up in flames, which he told friends about all of a month before the actual fire occurred.

Some of Harold's intuitions were more personal, entailing clear warnings. He used to help out in his brother's fish-and-chip shop in the evenings; one day a man came in who made Harold feel extremely uncomfortable – he told his brother there was something evil about him. His brother scoffed, but a few weeks later Harold came across a photograph of the man in a newspaper: he had been arrested for attempting to poison his fellow employees.

On another occasion, Harold saw a man sitting in the back of a truck parked in a side road near the chip shop; he was dressed in working clothes and wore a flat cap. He, too, instilled in Harold a feeling of terrible discomfort. Harold saw him several times, and each time felt uneasy. Then one evening, after leaving his brother in the shop, he began to feel very ill at ease. He went back and found the man in the back yard, about to enter at the rear. Harold approached him and persuaded him to leave. His next sight of him was in a newspaper photograph; it seemed that this man had committed a series of brutal murders in London. By following his intuitive feeling, Harold had quite possibly saved his brother's life.

One of the mysteries about premonitions is that they are not always as useful as this. They may be about something quite insignificant, while failing to touch on events which are much more important. One acquaintance of mine had a premonitory dream about a blocked bath-plug, but was given no forewarning of his marriage breakdown and divorce. He did, however, have three dreams about falling off his motorbike during the weeks before he actually did fall off. It could be wise to take note of premonitions about accidents, even though this does not necessarily prevent them from happening.

It is frustrating to foresee an accident about which one can do nothing. I used to attend an annual festival of transport held on a private estate in Northamptonshire at which my Aikido club gave demonstrations. One year, one of the spectacles was a bungee jump. One jumper was just preparing, when in my mind I saw him hit the ground. Only a few moments later he was making the jump, and there was nothing I could do except to distract my young son so that he didn't witness the fall. (Fortunately, we found out later that the victim had survived.)

Even when we see disasters that are unpreventable, there may be a reason and even a benefit. It is normal for our subconscious mind to look at potential situations and take us through scenarios of our possible responses, using dreams and day-dreams as a kind of rehearsal for real life. After a premonition, even a subtle one, we are able to practise coping with the forth-coming situation in the same way, so that we are prepared for the impact of the event when it comes, and can act more construc-tively.

By no means all precognition consists of warnings or relates to tragic events. Sometimes both dreams and visions seem to be sent to reassure or encourage us. Some of my own dreams have foreseen good news for other people, such as the birth of a child for a good friend who believed she was unable to have children. However, it would seem that the most memorable examples are likely to be both powerful and personal. Among historical fig-ures, Napoleon Bonaparte is reported to have had dreams of his future success long before there was any indication of the posi-tion of power that he would hold.

It is often the quality of these dreams or visions that holds them in our memory. My mother once had a dream that made no sense to her at the time, but she remembered it because it felt unusual and was so puzzling. She could see herself as though from above, in a room she didn't recognise, where she was work-ing with other people on some kind of equipment. She also saw the outside of the building and a long corridor.

At the time my mother didn't work and had no plans for a change of circumstance. When she and my father separated, however, everything changed. Within a year she decided to go back to school, and after passing her GCEs she applied to a teachers' training college. At her interview, she recognised from her dream the outside of the building and the corridor. When she actually started her course and found herself doing an exper-iment in a science lab, the rest fell into place. She was quite startled; the total accuracy of her prophetic dream so long ago was undeniable.

The dream had been telling my mother of a major turning point in her life. She had left school at fourteen, and had had to abandon her education. Now, in her mid-thirties, everything changed. Eventually she acquired a degree and post-graduate qualifications as well as a satisfying teaching career. She also became self-sufficient and able to support her family as a single parent.

In a similar vein, for about five years before I began to search for my past-life family I used to have dreams of being interviewed. I actually hoped that these dreams were not going to come true, because being in the limelight has never been my idea of fun; I chose instead to look upon them as a way of clarifying my thoughts. But when *Yesterday's Children* was published I found myself giving many interviews, and all of a sudden those nocturnal rehearsals made sense.

From the point of view of validating precognitive experiences, it is obviously useful when they can be shared before the event. Some years ago I dreamed that I was driving my husband's car, an old Austin A35, in Northampton. Trying to turn right at traffic lights, I couldn't engage any gear and was stuck in the outside lane, blocking the traffic. Then a truck driver helped me push the car up on to the pavement, after which I walked to Steve's place of work. When we returned to the car it only took a few moments to put it right, and I laughed with relief that it was not something major.

When I awoke from this very detailed dream I told Steve about it and joked that, knowing me, it would probably all happen. At that time Steve was not working in Northampton and I had my own car. Four months later my car developed a fault; Steve had been transferred to a job in Northampton, so we shared his car and arranged that I should pick him up from work. I forgot about my dream until I reached the Bedford Road traffic lights and, positioned in the outside lane ready to turn right, discovered that I couldn't engage any gear. A truck driver came to my rescue as I just sat there, taking in the fact that I had dreamed every detail exactly as it was now happening.

As to why I should have dreamed all this in advance, this is one of the many unanswered questions in this area. But from a personal point of view, it all adds to a body of experience that helps me to trust in the accuracy of my other visions of the future, even the far distant future which cannot be verified so easily.

How accurate can visions of the future be? In virtually all experiments into psychic phenomena the degree of accuracy is variable; even the very best subjects give some pieces of information that are not truly psychic. Professor J. B. Rhine of Duke University in North Carolina, a noted early researcher into psychic phenomena, found that subjects achieved much better results in a conducive atmosphere, free of all outside distractions. But even under ideal circumstances not every single detail would be completely right.

In fairness this should be compared to the degree of accuracy that we can expect from the mind in connection with other functions such as memory. Nobody has perfect recall of every moment of their lives, and in remembering an event in detail we introduce errors by trying to fill in the gaps. In visions of the future, inaccuracies also occur when people put their own interpretation on what they are seeing.

About ten years ago I was at a family gathering and felt in the right mood to sense the future. I decided to concentrate on each person in turn, trying to see them as they would look when they got older. I saw my younger brother as a slightly heavier man with white hair at the temples: he is now beginning to acquire some white hair and carries a bit of extra weight. But Michael did not appear to age at all; try as I might to see his older self, while everyone else changed he did not. I concluded, mistakenly, that he would not change with age. It wasn't until his death a few years later that the real reason became clear. What this demonstrates is that trying to make sense of something one doesn't understand can lead one into making incorrect interpretations.

In fact, when I have premonitory dreams or waking glimpses of the future I am usually fairly certain that they will happen. These precognitive experiences always have the same quality as the memory of an event that has already happened. Rather than seeing a future that has not yet happened, it feels more like picking up an event that has already been set in time – just like a memory but thrown back in time rather than forward.

In my experience, the link between an event as it happens and precognition of that event is the quality of my own reaction. Both the moment of foreseeing and the moment of experiencing the event in its true time tend to be accompanied by an odd feeling, a kind of mental jolt. It is as though the mind exists simultaneously at two different points in time, but connected with itself and functioning across time instead of just in the present. Another way to put it is that it is almost as though time has folded at that point and become one experience instead of two. Frequently my mind is in a relaxed and receptive condition at both points in time.

A possible explanation for this was originally suggested to me by my son. We look at time from the present moment; we see the past behind us and the future ahead, and think of ourselves existing in the now. But this linear view itself may limit our understanding of time and of the mind. Perhaps precognition involves a kind of telepathic communication across time.

There have been enough scientific tests of telepathy for this to be accceptable as a real and valid phenomenon. Telepathy requires both a sender and a receiver. In scientific experiments the sending of a mental message is deliberate, but in ordinary life telepathic communication between family members (and often between pets and their owners) occurs spontaneously, particularly at times of high emotion.

Could precognition of events in this or future lives involve a similar process, so that the information is passed, usually unknowingly, from a future sender to a receiver in the present? Certainly I feel that at least some instances of precognition involve a connection with one's future self, or the person whose future one is 'seeing'. I certainly feel that kind of connection when I see myself with an old face. (I look forward to having white hair, and looking back at these times.) Foresight of a less personal nature may well require two future minds or more.

Most people's premonitions, including my own, tend to be concerned with small, personal events. Useful predictions are much more unusual. This may be partly due to the fact that day-to-day happenings generally affect our lives more than world events. It is possible that a seer like Nostradamus, who foresaw many events of significant social importance, may have been accessing the minds of numbers of other people through time.

Can everyone see the future? The people who make use of psychic ability within their lives are usually born with a natural psychic gift which they develop over time through trial and error. But I believe that many more people could access that unexercised part of their mind, or spirit. There is nothing magic or mystical about *psi*, nor is it anything to do with religious belief. It can be an ordinary part of life and a natural means of communication or understanding. As with all human abilities, some people will be good at it and find it easy, while others will have to work at it, and a few might find it very difficult.

How can we see the future? Perhaps the first thing to do is accept the possibility that we can. One thing that is fairly certain is that it is a right-brain activity. These days most people are trained through their education to enhance left-brain functions, like step-by-step reasoning and the use of language, and are actively discouraged from day-dreaming. But reflective and intuitive feelings use more of the right side of the brain, the area which is probably responsible for the sudden creative leaps that people sometimes make when problem solving.

My father used to wake up in the middle of the night and write down all sorts of mathematical equations that came to him quite suddenly. This is more than likely to have been due to his using right-brain intuition, which is often easier to reach when one is not trying in a conscious or analytical way, but gently musing on a problem in a state of rest and relaxation such as just before sleep.

Because few people are able to achieve a deep state of relaxation while awake, a good start would be to make a point of noting your dreams. It is true that most dreams are to do with everyday life, and prophetic dreams are relatively rare. But regularly taking notice of our dreams enables us to become aware of those that are meaningful. It is helpful to remind yourself before going to sleep that you intend to remember your dreams, and to keep a notebook or tape recorder by your bed so that you can record them before they slip away.

To become open to waking visions of the future, it is necessary to cultivate a state of mind that encourages right-brain activity. People who have psychic episodes frequently may be doing nothing more unusual than allowing themselves to experience that very subtle state which combines relaxation with mental alertness and concentration. For those to whom this does not come naturally, meditation is a good way of cultivating that state of mind. The same day-dreamy, reflective, meditative state is evident in all kinds of psychic experience. It is also a state in which the level of concentration and mental activity is very high. Children under the age of six frequently produce similar brain-wave frequencies to those found in people who have spent many years learning how to meditate effectively. This is worth noting, because it is before the age of six that children are also more likely to remember past lives.

It is perhaps important to note here that it is extremely unwise to use drugs to induce trance states. Quite apart from the obvious dangers, anything you might see would be unlikely to be reliable or of any use, and the required level of concentration would in any case be impaired by drugs or alcohol. I personally find it helpful to be teetotal.

If we are to look for artificial aids, it is known that physical stimulation of different areas of the brain can prompt memories as well as other senses, and under experimental conditions stimulation of the right temporal lobe has been found to induce out-of-body experiences. Perhaps similar experiments could also be used to induce precognition as more is learned about brain activity.

Precognitive abilities are more than usually apparent in a number of the people who have been through a near-death experience. It is known that the more you use a particular nerve pathway, the better it functions. It is possible that NDEs stimulate the brain into developing hitherto unused nerve pathways, enabling psychic experiences to happen more easily. There is a lot still to be discovered about the links between the mind, our overall awareness and the brain, which the mind uses as a living machine to process information.

When Nostradamus made his predictions, they were rarely clear-cut but consisted of small snapshots, like pieces of a jigsaw. From my point of view, this actually makes his prophecies far stronger and more likely than if they were complete, simply because this is exactly how precognition seems to work. One does not see everything at one time and there is no real way to choose what will be seen. Sometimes quite important pieces are missed out, and visions come randomly with no sense of order in time.

To look into the future, Nostradamus would sit for hours meditating by candlelight on a shallow bowl of water, but many of his insights came unbidden. Meditation may have helped him to gain some of the detail he needed to understand what he saw, but some of his spontaneous visions contained enough information for him to be able to specify times and places. He went to great lengths to describe what he saw in as much detail as possible and from his own standpoint. However, his accounts are complicated by his need to protect himself from persecution by disguising the premonitions in cryptic verse. This has been the cause of both misinterpretations and rejection of his ability.

The main areas covered by Nostradamus's prophetic verse are the politics of war, and sometimes the tragedies of nature. This sort of subject matter is extremely useful as it can be identified, particularly as he was often able to name places and people, albeit cryptically, though not always dates. His skill was clearly exceptional.

Under hypnosis, when I came to look at a period forty years hence, I described Central Africa as being in a state of turmoil and northern China having a political strength that unsettled its neighbours. I later discovered that both of these situations are mentioned by Nostradamus, but in stronger terms. He describes a series of widespread and devastating wars, which tend to alarm people who fear all kinds of unpleasantness as we approach the end of the millennium.

However, these descriptions need to be seen in perspective. To Nostradamus a vision of the Gulf War, for example, could seem overwhelmingly destructive compared with the kind of warfare conducted in his own time. While the Gulf War was of course very destructive, it was not global. It could be, therefore, that the wars that Nostradamus predicts for our present and future are those that are already going on in different parts of the world – which are unpleasant and worrying but not so far affecting the whole planet.

One of his prophecies which appears to apply to the distant future struck a chord of recognition in me. Although Nostradamus spoke of a period of war, he predicted that this would be followed by a time of peace, when the population would be very much reduced. This is comparable with the future time that I have seen, with a much smaller world population, a sense of security and very little violence, if any: a time not just of freedom from war but of unusual civil harmony. So, while many people today see the world situation currently moving from bad to worse, it seems that there is real hope for the future of humanity and the planet.

CHAPTER 8

Nadia,
Tomorrow's Child

A future life

When I started to have random glimpses into what I could only explain as a future life, all my old feelings came into play about keeping the subject to myself and close friends only. For a few years I felt very cautious and self-conscious about it, simply because it was almost too strange to discuss. It was like being a child all over again. As a child I had to cope with my memories of a past life, knowing that reincarnation was not generally accepted. But now I was an adult, and I realised that the only way to find out whether I could explain, or even to some extent prove, this new phenomenon was to attempt to do so.

The first time that I saw, or rather felt, my tomorrow was during the Easter holiday of 1990. We were on a long homeward car journey from Eastbourne on the South Coast back to the Midlands, many hours after our early-morning outward trip. I sat in the passenger seat while Steve drove and our children lay exhausted in the back. The sun was low and shafts of brilliant light flickered between the trees, drawing my gaze. With my face turned west towards the setting sun, and enjoying the view of rolling fields bordered by large, still trees, I relaxed and allowed my mind to drift.

I was not asleep, and what happened next didn't feel like a dream, yet it was not of the present, not of the here and now. The first odd thing happened as I ran my fingers through my hair and was strangely aware that its texture had unexpectedly altered. I felt curious, knowing that this was hardly usual, but I was in no way alarmed. Instead of my usually thick, curly hair, the smooth strands under my fingers were fine, ending in little matted knots. I was immediately reminded of the way my children's hair used to feel, before the first haircut removed the feathery baby hair. At that point, and with considerable surprise, I noticed that although I could physically feel the hair that was not my own, my hands were still on my lap.

Obviously, something extremely out of the ordinary was going on. I looked at Steve and said, 'Just now something curious is happening. I'll tell you more about it in a minute.' I was still sufficiently aware of my surroundings to notice that he had put on a cassette tape of Mike and the Mechanics, which I later replaced with the *Missa Louba*, a spirited rendition of the Congalese mass sung by an African choir.

As the altered state continued it was as though I were two selves at once, temporarily occupying the same space as if superimposed on each other; I was aware first of one and then the other. I was also conscious that the new self belonged to another time. This other self was small, with darkish skin. She was an Asian girl of about two and was sitting on the ground in the open air, in the day-dreaming state of mind so common in young children.

Although the whole thing was very peculiar, for some reason I couldn't explain I felt certain that this was my future self. Almost instantaneously with seeing and feeling her, I accepted her as just that. I knew that she was called Nadia and that she was a part of me. There was no problem as far as I was concerned in accepting that she was nothing to do with my present lifetime; however improbable it might at first seem, I simply knew that Nadia was who I would be in my next life. I also felt, uniquely, that she was aware of me: that I was the self who was being remembered.

The trigger for this event may have been the success I was beginning to have at that stage with my research into my previous life. At that point in 1990 I had at last found the first written proof of Mary Sutton's existence, her death certificate, and I knew then that it might be possible to substantiate all my other memories of her. Knowing that this might give me the chance of talking openly about her at last was a source of tremendous relief.

It may also have given me the confidence to acknowledge that what I was seeing now could be beyond the end of my present life. In fact, I may have seen glimpses of this life before, but had either failed to recognise what they were or had suppressed them. My need to conform is quite strong, and my past-life memories were quite enough to cope with; it would have been hard before then to admit consciously to seeing visions of a future life. Also, for me to acknowledge these visions there had to be nothing vague about them. They had to be experienced in this dramatic and unambiguous way, while I was awake, and at a time when I was able to accept them for what they were. Because once I had accepted the experience, it could no longer be ignored: I would have to discuss it with others, understand it and somehow cope with it.

This experience of looking into the future had a different quality from remembering my past life as Mary. Those had been like any other memories; there was never anything strange about them. With this newer experience I felt that we were linked: I was living the feelings not so much as a memory, but as though I was in the past and two-year-old Nadia was remembering me from her life in the future, in the year 2040. Memory can be extremely vivid at times; one can recall and relive smells, sights, sounds and emotions. But this didn't feel relived or remembered; it felt alive, as if I were being touched by this future existence.

After that, it was as though I had opened a door through which ever more snatches of my future life would drift. Pictures and feelings would come to me at any time, like the fragments of memory that play constantly against the background of our everyday consciousness. In the same way that I remembered more about my past lives by spending time thinking about them consciously, so I now consciously encouraged the glimpses of the future that came to me. There was never any doubt in my mind that I was seeing my own future, starting around 2040. I was aware of the time period, somehow knowing it as a certainty, just as I had with my past-life memories. And it still felt like me but within a different body. Slowly I began to learn more.

The name Nadia was just there as a feeling, in much the same way as the name Mary had always been; I had no sense of a second name at that stage. Similarly I had an awareness of the location, which was fairly specific. Just as I had always known that Mary had lived in Ireland, I knew that Nadia lived in eastern Nepal. There was a place nearby whose name began with 'Dhar——', possibly followed by one or two more syllables which did not come to me.

Over time, as I opened my mind to Nadia's life, I gained more and more images. They came in snatches at different times, mostly while I was awake, but sometimes in a dream or semi-dream state. I had to build up the whole picture from small fragments which sometimes covered only a few details; these, however, were unfailingly consistent. Whenever I saw them, the village and landscape were always the same. In some ways it was similar to trying to piece together a half-forgotten memory, going over the clearer bits many times, and only gradually enlarging them with further peripheral glimpses.

Nadia's home was in a village set against a hillside in a mountainous area. A winding track led north out of the village; south of the track the land fell steeply into a valley, beyond which lay many more hills. Uphill to the south-east there was only the hillside rising. There were signs of regular heavy rainfall, as the narrow path around the hillside was eroded by rivulets that cut into the finely textured, reddish orange soil. This soil, a slightly sandy loam, reminded me of estuary mud. I could feel its fine, crumbly texture as the very young Nadia played with the damp mud after a rainfall; she could press it into a ball, but it soon broke apart.

Some of the neighbouring hillsides were heavily wooded, but the area near to the village consisted mainly of scrubland. Downhill I could see a gorge whose bottom was overgrown with virtual jungle; as I looked up the hillside rocky outcrops were visible. There were a few areas of flatter land – small clearings each containing two or three long, low, single-storey family houses. These were utilitarian, quite spartan and painted white, and their surroundings were kept very clean.

Nadia's home was in the northernmost clearing close to the path that wound around the hillside. There were more houses uphill and downhill, perhaps twenty altogether, at different levels but all lying to the south of the area that I had first seen. They were all family homes providing shelter for large extended families. The path leading out of the village dropped to cross a stony, dusty road and continued towards the fields.

The young Nadia seemed to be looked after during much of the day by an oldish woman who I thought might be her grandmother, and I felt that there were perhaps three older children in her family. As I sensed her growing up I was aware of high cheekbones and slightly narrowed eyes, which gave her face more of a Tibetan, slightly oriental look than traditional Indian Asian features.

I had a particularly clear picture of Nadia at about the age of sixteen. This was interesting because at one point I saw her as if from the outside, as well as experiencing being her. She was standing with some friends by a field, where a number of people seemed to be working. I saw a group of four young women, including Nadia, all dressed in a type of sari, perhaps not as full as the Indian sari, consisting of a plain bodice and a wrapped-around skirt. There was a great deal of self-conscious laughter as the group of girls were having their photograph taken, by an outsider it seemed. At one point I even saw what the finished photograph looked like. The names of Nadia's friends, as far as I could tell, were Sati, Tahera and possibly Neair.

I saw her too at a later age, now as a mother. She was working in what was probably the same large field, with a little boy of about three who ran barefoot, playing between the rows of crops. The feeling at this time was different, less relaxed and more demanding; Nadia seemed concerned about something, perhaps an illness. I was squatting close to the ground, probably weeding the crop; it was hard to tell what the wispy shoots would grow into, but it looked like some kind of cereal. There may have been other women in the field, but they were not close enough at that moment to talk to.

I knew that this vision of the distant future was going to be virtually impossible to verify in my own lifetime. But some aspects of the area she lived in could be checked out, since they would probably remain unchanged – including the type of soil and the geography of the area. There was certainly some scope for research.

When I had researched my past life as Mary in Ireland my quest was to trace the children about whom I was so anxious, which meant locating the home that I remembered. This I was able to do because not only were there surviving buildings and landmarks but most of the children were still living. My quest for the future was going to be quite different; it also demanded the courage to start what has to be seen as a very peculiar line of study.

First I had to draw a map of the area, and to research any tiny detail that might lead to locating it accurately; this would include detailed descriptions of any building that might already be standing now. Since none of the land seemed flat, drawing a map of the village was going to be demanding. The ideal course would have been to travel to Nepal to look for the village, once I was fairly certain of its location. But even without the cost involved, it was not a journey I could make. Due to a variety of serious allergies I had acquired during a period of stress, there are a number of places where I am unable to travel; one of them is Nepal.

I decided to start by checking on both the area and Nepalese names. Looking in an atlas at a poorly detailed map of Nepal, I found that the area that felt right was confined to a fairly limited

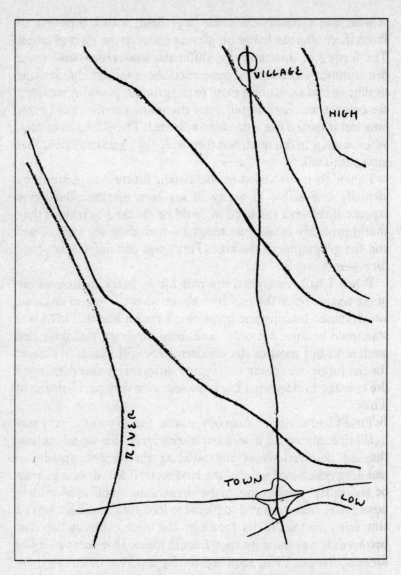

My first sketch map of the area near Nadia's village.

region in the east of the country, halfway between Mount Everest in the north and the border with India in the south. There was only one town named in the atlas, Dhankuta, which fitted well with the partial name I already had. But I really needed to find a more detailed map. As for the name Nadia, after attempting some research I heard a letter read out on the breakfast television programme from a Nadia with an Asian surname, so I knew that this was a possible name for a Nepalese girl.

Before looking at more detailed maps or doing any more research, I felt it was important for me to learn as much as possible about the future life itself. If I waited for further visions, it could take a long time to gather enough information to pinpoint the actual village. However, there was one method which might enable me to gain fuller details more speedily. I decided to try a further experiment in hypnosis.

In some ways this research would not be unlike the experience of looking at past lives, but my fears were very different. Looking into the past and finding there a cause of emotional trauma, facing it and coming to terms with it, can bring about a sense of relief and healing. But to look at the future, knowing that whatever is seen there has yet to be faced, could have quite a different effect and might possibly become a cause of anguish. This in itself was a genuine anxiety which I had to take into consideration.

I did not initially question whether it was possible to see into the future whilst under hypnosis; I think I took it for granted. I had had many visions of the future while in a rested state; it must be feasible, I thought, for the same thing to happen under hypnosis. Looking back, my optimism on this point could be seen as almost reckless! But my need to search for the future had become urgent, though in a very different way from my search for my past.

One thing I was in no doubt about at all was that I was genuinely seeing a real future. All my visions of the future seen in dreams had later been realised as actual events. It is less common for me to see visions while awake, but when I do they tend to include a high proportion of accurate detail, even when covering a long time period; again, they have always happened. Visions seen through concentration techniques tend to be less accurate in detail and sometimes harder to interpret. But with all these methods I had at some point been able to tell other people of future events that did eventually come about. So I trusted my future visions.

With the use of hypnosis I hoped to gain the same sort of experience found through spontaneous premonition or active concentration; I had already discovered that, with someone else in control, results could be achieved far more easily, and I hoped to gain additional details as I had when recalling Mary's life under hypnosis.

Once I had made my decision I wrote to Jim Alexander, who had helped me with the regression hypnosis as part of my past-life research. It was five years since those sessions, but we had already discovered that the subconscious trigger which would induce in me an instant hypnotic state was still in place. We had reconstructed a hypnotic session for the *Strange But True?* series for London Weekend Television, for which I was not expected or asked to go into a real trance. But with only a very brief instruction I had reached a hypnotised condition almost immediately.

I was not sure whether Jim would be able to help me to look at the future or even whether he would think it prudent to try, but I did know that I could trust him and would feel safe with him in charge. I also knew that there had been some previous experimentation into hypnotic progression – the term for seeing the future under hypnosis. The hypnotist Albert de Roches, whose early research into regression hypnosis was published in 1903, claimed that some of his patients seemed able to see into future lives under hypnosis.

Progression is not generally considered a useful subject of study, since the distant future cannot be proved and there is a great deal of scope for the imagination to come into play. However, because I had already indicated the period in question and had a history of accurate precognition, I felt there was a stronger case for research than usual. Jim and I met to discuss what was happening to me, and he agreed to try hypnotic progression. In October 1993 we embarked on a series of seven experimental sessions.

Although I had thought myself well prepared to undergo hypnosis again I must have had some unconscious anxiety, because at first I found myself struggling a little and holding on to conscious control. But after that I slowly drifted first into a light trance, then gradually into a deeper state. As my body became limp I recognised that sinking sensation, a little like drifting off to sleep yet without ever falling asleep completely. My conscious mind was left behind with my body, able to observe but no longer in control.

Soon Jim's disembodied voice was once again directing me. He instructed me not to use my imagination but only to describe what I experienced, using all of my senses. At first there was only the voice, and then I was guided through the world of the sub-conscious. Jim asked me to see time passing, and I saw a con-stantly shifting and changing series of pictures at a distance, a little like a strip of film held against a dark wall. Then I was drawn ahead into the future, still watching the pictures but as yet unable to focus clearly on any particular one.

Jim's voice told me to find the year 2050 and I plunged invol-untarily towards a point in time when I knew myself as Nadia, at the age of eight, in the village I was already familiar with. On this occasion, a dry and warm time of year, a number of women and children were doing something with a grain crop. I could see a flat stone about 18 inches across, though I was not sure what it was used for – it did not seem to be for grinding. Although ostensibly helping, I and the other children were really playing, and even the women who were doing the job seemed to be relaxed and smiling rather than worn down by work.

The voice, which part of me still knew belonged to Jim, asked me my surname and I came up with something that sounded like 'Tanchan'. As he questioned me about my life, I mentioned three older sisters and a younger brother. Then he asked what I could tell him about local and world news. The picture changed. I saw myself at a different time in the streets of the nearby town, listening to people talking; the main topic was the repeated flooding that had recently affected an area far to the south outside Nepal. (After the session I felt that the location may have been the Ganges delta around Calcutta.) The questioning continued throughout; usually my answers were quite brief. Sometimes the answer would take me to a different view, a different day.

'Do you read any newspapers?'

I looked for a newspaper. There was a small dropside truck that came to collect surplus grain; the surly driver, who didn't ever bother to get out of his cab to help with the loading, would engross himself in a newspaper while he waited. He appeared to be Indian rather than Nepalese.

'What other vehicles are there?'

I answered that there were only a few, which mainly passed through the village on their way between towns. There were a few traders, one of whom sold sandals for 24, or perhaps 240 or 2400, of some unnamed currency (my self in the present knew that these were rupees). This trader used to load a mule or donkey with his wares, so that the animal seemed to be decorated with multicoloured sandals. There was also a very battered vehicle, possibly a minibus, that could take children to school and others into the town; it ran to a highly unpredictable timetable.

Asked to describe money, I found myself looking at three round coins made of different types of alloy. In particular I noted a silvery coin covered extensively in ornate Indian-style characters. It was fairly small, about the size of a British 5p coin, and thin – the edges seemed almost sharp. I could not quite make out whether it had a hole in the centre; this uncertainty made me wonder if some other coins did. I knew that the truck driver exchanged notes with the men of the village, but I did not see them.

The nearest town was a few miles away to the south-west. I named it as Dhankuta, but afterwards felt that this was wrong; after looking at the map I had decided that the village was north of Dhankuta, but Dhankuta was probably much further away than the small town I described. It had narrow streets, paved unevenly with stones slightly larger than a standard brick. Only some of the streets were wide enough for the few vehicles; most were either too narrow or too cluttered. Most of the vehicles passed through on the north–south road; few took the road east which led back to Nadia's village.

In the middle of one roadway stood a decorative structure of some sort, perhaps a well, and many of the buildings had objects attached to their eaves, overhanging the street. Some of these may have been goods for sale, but some, I felt, were talismans or some kind of good luck tokens. The streets didn't appear particularly crowded, but there was a continual stream of people, most walking fairly slowly and taking their time about whatever they were doing.

When Jim asked me to go forward ten years I found myself aged eighteen, in the middle of a marriage ceremony. It was the first time that there had been any sense of seriousness in this otherwise delightfully carefree existence. I was happy at getting married, but my prime emotion seems to have been a sense of pride at the prestige of my new, grown-up status.

The groom was a very young-looking man who came from our village; I gave his name as Ghunta – reluctantly, as I always had difficulty with names in these sessions. The ceremony was being held in a very ornate building in the town, and was expected to take all day. An elderly priest, apparently absorbed in his task, stood before us. I described my clothes as layered; I was aware of the unaccustomed weight of several layers of a loose, possibly long-sleeved garment, decorated at the edges. My husband was in white trousers and a loose tunic; again his clothing seemed to involve several layers. Jim asked whether alcohol would be consumed at the celebrations and my reply expressed severe disapproval; I said I hoped that there would be no alcohol!

Now Jim asked me simply to drift in time until drawn to some event. I saw once again the group of young women being photographed near the fields when I was about sixteen. I could see letters on the camera, the first few of which were 'Nic'. The photographers were tourists, foreigners who seemed very large in comparison to us; they were possibly American. I couldn't help giggling at their serious manner, as well as their heavy boots and safari-style suits. We wore sandals to walk on the steep paths, but they needed big boots! This was the cause of great mirth which made sense at the time, though the significance was lost on me when I was no longer hypnotised.

The photograph was taken at the south end of a field fairly near to a stone-built shrine, which was highly decorated in both intricate stonework and more temporary materials and may have had amulets hanging from it. The structure made me think of an English folly; it looked like a façade, only about 2 feet in depth, with side walls and a pitched roof.

When it was time for me to return to the present I was in a fairly deep state of trance. However, once awake, I wanted to discuss everything while it was still fresh. Although the sessions were being recorded, I knew from previous experience that it was essential to discuss what I had seen or write it down fairly soon or many of the details would return to my subconscious to be forgotten. This was especially true of things seen for the first time, or under very deep hypnosis. And this single first session had produced an amazing amount of new detail.

Because it was so easy to see things under hypnosis I had a very slight qualm that not everything might be real or accurate, yet at the same time I was quite certain that Nadia was a reality, my future self. What I had not expected was my tremendous sense of relief. Perhaps I had been afraid that the simple life I expected to find might also be full of hardship, but this was not the case. I was left with a feeling of a terrific zest for life and enjoyment of every little facet of living. Although it was a fairly basic existence, there was no sense of lack. Even the knowledge that my education and opportunities would be limited in this future did not diminish my sheer delight. There was a richness and warmth in companionship that remained in my consciousness, brightening the present, and for several days afterwards I felt very relaxed and cheerful.

A week later, back in Jim's large reclining chair, I found myself listening once more to his gentle but persistent direction as it led me into the realms of my subconscious mind. The first stop was as Nadia at the age of twenty. Perhaps because I was tired that day, or because of the mood of the time we had reached, I spoke little at first.

I was inside a single-storey house; it was fairly new, and there were indications that it was not quite completed. It had no partition walls and, although the total living area for the family was only about 10 by 20 feet (3 by 6 m), it felt roomy and airy. The sense of space was probably due in part to the sparsity of the furniture. There were a bed, a cot and a few household items placed against one wall. I was looking out of a square window about 2 feet (60 cm) across which had roughly finished concrete reveals, painted white. In the cot slept a baby girl, Nadia's first child. It was early morning and all was quiet and still.

When Jim questioned me I found it difficult to speak coherently and answered with only a few words at a time. I told him that the men of the village had gone early that morning to work on a project to do with water. I was aware that an outside organisation was using local labour for development schemes. This meant that there was well-paid work, but I wasn't sure what they were building or why. I concluded afterwards that the project may have been a hydroelectricity plant.

Next I was asked to identify any buildings of importance in the town. I found the shops interesting, but only the temple and the government offices were important. Part of the offices were used by Americans, who were there with government support, but among the local people there was uncertainty and a touch of apprehension about what they were doing. To some extent this was due to our natural concern over imminent change and unfamiliarity with these foreigners who were so different from ourselves. Once I came out of hypnosis I found it more difficult to identify with the sense of uncertainty, but it seemed to be associated with a culture which saw itself as one large family.

Then Jim asked me to look twenty years ahead, when Nadia would be forty. There was nothing there. I experienced a kind of shock. For a brief spell I felt as if I were teetering on the edge of a precipice; then I was being drawn back to the present and the large chair in which my motionless body reclined, separated from my mind in a peculiar limbo.

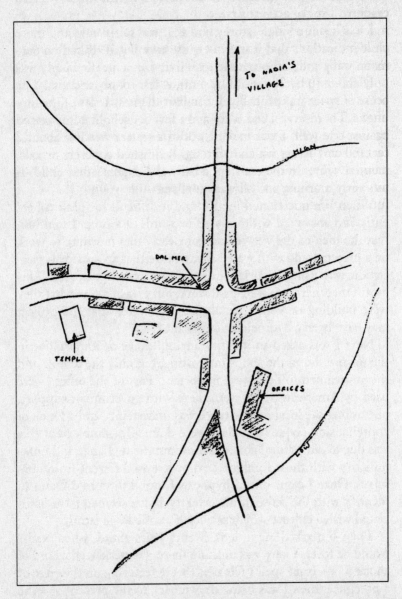

A sketch map of the town near Nadia's village, showing positions of various buildings of importance.

Perhaps the instant of shock at realising that Nadia no longer existed at forty had retriggered the fears that had dominated so much of my life – the fear of dying too young and anxiety for my children's safety. Jim asked me to go back ten years, but at that moment I was unable to do so or see anything more.

For a while afterwards I was quite disturbed by this. I had been concerned about how I might feel if I saw anything unpleasant in my future using hypnosis. However, I had in the past received forewarning of difficult times, and had managed to carry on day-to-day without too much concern. This had helped me to acquire a kind of emotional detachment regarding precognition, and it wasn't too long before I was able to apply this to my future as Nadia.

CHAPTER 9

The Quest
for Nadia

Looking at Nepal

In our third session, Jim took me back to my early childhood in this life, asking me to recount my first day at school and then to look at an event which occurred at the age of ten. Both of these turned out unexpectedly to be extremely upsetting. This was certainly not the intention. Jim's purpose was to get me to look at past events that were easily identifiable as real, since this would help to validate the reality of my other experiences while under hypnosis.

Returning to these memories, I became totally overwhelmed by intense emotions which had not really bothered me since leaving my childhood behind. Such is the effect of hypnosis that it was as though I was there, once more a vulnerable child, and I was unable to hold back the tears as I described events that normally no longer upset me. I, as observer, could not override the emotions; all I could do was remember and listen to the child within, talking about pains long past.

It was not in fact my first day at school that I remembered but the day when I missed the early school bus and had to catch the second one. The local primary school had not yet been built, so the five-year-old children were taken by bus to an old, Victorian-style school in the town several miles away. It was a temporary arrangement and I felt that the teachers were as unhappy with it as we were. I was terrified of my teacher and feared punishment for missing the first bus, so it was not surprising that memory came to the fore. (I was not in fact punished for being late, but my teacher was angry at my timidity when I tried to explain my lateness.)

The other event I relived was the time when my father dismantled and destroyed our sledge in his anger, because I had taken a small piece of wood that he wanted and used it as a seat. My own anger and frustration mingled with the fear that was a regular childhood accompaniment to my father's wrath.

Distressing though these memories were, the net effect was that, when I was then taken to Nadia's life at the age of twenty-five, I found it a lot easier to describe what was there without the recurrent uncertainty of my present self getting in the way. My inhibitions had been removed, pulling away the threads of consciousness which occasionally acted as a censor and hampered my ability to communicate. This time my answers were less stilted and more complete.

Jim asked me a number of questions relating to the distance away of the town south-west of the village, and how often Nadia went there. I answered that it was within walking distance but easier to reach by bus. This would make it less than 10 miles (16 km) away, most likely only about 4 (6km). About once a month we made trips there which frequently coincided with religious festivals – there were two or three major festivals a year and a number of lesser ones.

In the town there was a temple which had a wide-angled pitched roof and decoration along the front edge which was carved in stone and consisted of many identical three-part pieces, a little like fleurs-de-lys, with spherical tops. Standing on the south side of the main street at a slight angle to the road, it was not new and is the building most likely to be found in the town today. Most of the other buildings in the centre were single- or occasionally double-storey shops or houses.

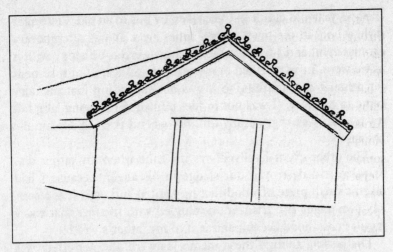

A sketch of the decoration I saw on the edge of the temple roof.

When asked what I bought at the shops, I said that most shops sold things that we didn't need (or more likely couldn't afford, and so managed without). The goods on sale were mainly locally made and the people who usually bought them were 'the people who pass through'. This suggested tourists, but I had a strong feeling that much was sold to the increasing number of American development workers who were billeted in the new government buildings at the south-east end of the town centre.

Jim asked if I read newspapers and what was in the news. I said that there were newspapers, but usually you could find out what was going on by talking with people. I felt that in any case there was little opportunity to read.

'What do people talk about?'

There were two important topics at that time. The first was a hold-up at the work site outside the town to the west. 'They are building a wall to slow down the water – there is a lot of water there. And they are making a machine there, but some of the parts haven't arrived and the men have nothing to do.'

It still seemed likely that this was a hydroelectric plant. It was the main project being developed with outside help, though I had the feeling that other projects were under way further afield.

As to world news, I was aware that Central Africa was going through turbulent times, but the other main subject of conversation was China, which of course concerned me more. The news was something to do with power and governments, but there was a background fear that whatever was going on threatened our stability. With this situation came a feeling of acceptance of the American development group and foreign help that had not previously been universal. Suddenly it felt comforting to have someone from a powerful country involved benevolently with Nepal. Afterwards, I wondered about this. Neighbouring Tibet was of course taken over by China in the 1950s; Nadia was speaking from the 2060s. Could China still be posing a threat over a hundred years ahead?

One difficulty with this kind of question was that the subjects that interested Nadia were the same that interest me, which is what I would expect since I believe that we are the same individual. From the point of view of research, however, this could be problematic at times, since our interests do not usually include the news. I tend to find out what is going on in the world only if I happen to see the television news in passing. If someone else has bought a newspaper I will look at it, and I listen to radio discussions when driving, but at home I am happy to be busy in silence.

This same casual approach in a country where there is much less instant access to news anyway would limit one's awareness of the world at large. Without television or newspapers, and with a limited education, most people would have little idea of what was going on. This is exactly how it was as Nadia; unless someone happened to talk about world or even local events, she would have no idea of what was going on. Unfortunately this limits the possibilities of forecasting wider future events. I had guessed beforehand that most of the details revealed through questions under hypnosis would be personal or parochial, and that was pretty much how it was turning out.

Before leaving the town I was asked to remember the street layout and any names. The only name I could see was 'Dal mer' written on a sign at the edge of the main street, and of course my knowledge of roads was limited to the routes on which Nadia travelled.

Another thing I observed in this session was the ease with which a mother could leave her children in the care of parents or in-laws in order to travel about. Possibly there are people who find this easy in Western communities, but here families often live considerable distances apart, which makes such arrangements difficult. In addition, many Western mothers are rather guilt-ridden; they see child-care as their sole responsibility and find it difficult to leave their children, even with family members, without feeling obliged to rush back as soon as possible.

The social arrangements in this future in Nepal (and very likely in present-day Nepal) were completely different. A child was not the total responsibility of the mother, or even of both parents, but could as easily be cared for by any member of the family; this was made easier because the families lived close to each other. It was expected that the younger women would work in the fields, leaving children with older relatives, and my very first vision of Nadia had been as a child accompanied by her grandmother. Now I described to Jim how, at the age of twenty-five, I had to go to the fields with other women because there had been a lot of rain and weeds were growing among the crops.

'Has there been flooding?' Jim's voice asked.

'No!' Nadia replied in a don't-be-so-silly tone of voice.

The village was built on a hill, so the worst that the rain could do was to wash down soil or small rocks from higher up. This made a mess of the paths and road from time to time, but rain was not considered a major problem. In general the weather felt mild, although there were seasonal changes. But despite the mildness, it seemed to be wet quite a lot of the time.

My clothing felt like cotton and was fairly fine, of a shirt-weight fabric, some having a slub to the thread or seed within the fibre producing a slight texture and irregularity to the fabric. This time I was able to give a better description of the food. There was a small, round, flat loaf made from ground grain, and a boiled dish of several types of grain and pulses which I described as good to eat. Occasionally there was fruit, but it tended to be seasonal; one fruit looked a bit like an over-large fig.

After this session I was determined to embark on drawing a map of the town and to try to gain as much detail as possible in future sessions. But to continue, knowing how hard it was going to be to prove anything, demanded all my reserves of stubborn perseverance.

The next time we met, Jim tried to encourage me to come up with useful or descriptive data. The difficulty was that, as Nadia, I had such a laid-back attitude to life that although I was seeing quite a lot. I couldn't be bothered to answer his questions! I had to tell him afterwards what I had seen.

On this occasion he asked me again about what we bought, about the types of food available, and whether we kept animals. The food was consistently a mixture of grains and pulses, with little variation. I saw a bird sitting in a nearby tree, its feathers an iridescent black which reflected green and purple in the sunlight; it was reminiscent of a mynah bird, with a similarly shrill call. There were some small chickens or bantams which may have been semi-wild, wandering through the village scavenging grain. I also saw some small children playing a game that consisted of throwing stones into squares scratched in the earth.

Next, we returned to my wedding day. It took up the whole day from the early-morning start, almost at first light, when the village people gathered round a cart drawn by a pony or donkey and walked to the town. This was a slow process, as it was a fair distance. I was aware of a number of priests or monks in the town; some were in pale robes, but those that Nadia considered more important were dressed in a dark colour. I had some difficulty describing everything, as my mind also picked up images of other ceremonies in Nadia's life, making it hard to pick out which details were relevant and which were superimposed from other memories, both Nadia's and of other weddings in other times. I had had the same problem when trying to remember Mary Sutton's wedding in Ireland.

Meanwhile, tiny flashes of Nadia's life were coming to me

quite often without either hypnosis or deliberate meditation, and this possible future life began to take on a fuller dimension as more fragments were added to the picture. There was one particular scene that recurred quite often, when I found myself continually focussing on a particular few moments on one particular day; it was as if those few moments drew me back again and again. I was standing at home looking out of the window, doing nothing, just looking and somehow waiting. My first child, a girl, was in her cot; nobody else was in the house. Several parts of the building were still not quite completed, but this was not too important.

I could envisage the inside wall so vividly at times that the uneven texture of the unplastered stone was fixed within my consciousness. There was only one window on the long back wall, which faced north-west towards the road, and a couple more in the opposite wall where the door was. Leaning against a wall was a kind of scythe, which suggested that at least one type of crop had to be cut by hand.

Standing there, looking out across the village, I could see the land drop away steeply towards the road. A number of small trees grew on the steep, rocky slopes between the different levels of houses, and away in the distance there was a forest. Looking out of the window to my right I could see many miles of undulating open land; far away, the hills grew into mountains and the distant woodlands looked dark against the land.

This house was one level higher up the hillside than the parental home, which was a short distance to the south. Whereas that first home was sheltered against the hillside and the view limited by its position close to a wooded gorge, the newer house felt high and exposed. Above it, the hillside became too steep for any further buildings to be put up.

What seemed significant about this scene was Nadia's frame of mind: I was aware of a calm, meditative, almost resigned feeling. It was also the kind of state that I recognised as conducive to psychic or spiritual experiences. Perhaps that was why I kept touching into this time frame, experiencing this tiny moment across time and across two lives.

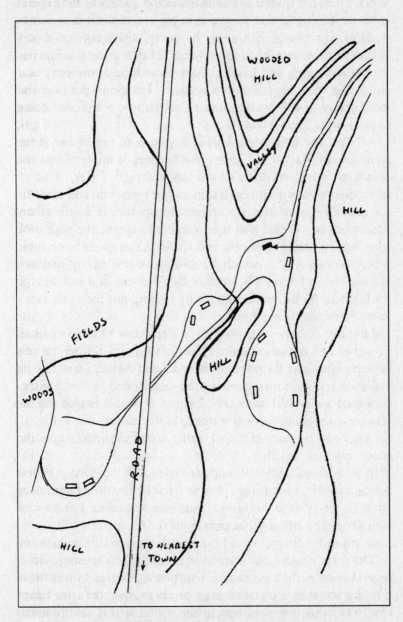

A more detailed sketch map of the area surrounding Nadia's home.

When I first felt myself as Nadia it was the quality of the experience, the intensity, that lodged it in my consciousness as something of significance. But under hypnosis, which assisted access
to the subconscious, I had no real sense of strangeness; it just felt
like remembering and talking about something as ordinary as a
childhood schoolday. Between sessions, I couldn't get over the
incongruity of this totally unusual adventure, which felt quite
natural while I was living it.

As with the time when I used hypnosis to remember more
about life as Mary, I did have some feelings of uncertainty, and
constantly questioned the details that emerged. Later I read of
other cases of hypnotic regression and progression, and came to
the conclusion that this is a common response. It is only when
details can be verified that it is possible to accept the reality of
what is seen under hypnosis, and that was not going to be easy.
There was no way in which I could prove objectively that my
visions were of a real future life. But I could find out what I
could about Nepal, including trying to pinpoint the exact location of Nadia's village home.

I did not embark on this research until after I had completed
my series of hypnosis sessions. Through Alf and Teresa, friends
of Steve who have friends in both India and Nepal, I was able to
order a large-scale map covering the eastern end of the country.
I awaited its arrival anxiously, hoping it would enable me to
recognise the village. I was warned, however, that this is one of
the least-visited parts of Nepal, and maps of the area frequently
show very little detail.

In mid-March 1994 the map arrived (see frontispiece). When
we collected it, I mentioned to our friends the coins I had seen;
later Alf was able to find some coins very like them. I also asked
him about the amulets hanging from the shrine in Nadia's village and in the town; he told me that this was a Hindu custom.

The map, which I had wanted to see since first sensing Nadia
several years earlier, contained a surprising degree of information. I was trying to do two things, pretty much at the same time.
One was to use my intuition to see which area drew me most
strongly; the other was to look for a long, fairly narrow valley

bordered on one side by a steep ridge of hills and on the other by a river, with enough flattish land for the large field I knew to be there. There would be a road or track heading up the valley towards a town – the one we visited. The town itself would be very close to the river, which looped around it; there had to be at least four routes out of it, the main one from the south, probably from Dhankuta.

Looking at it from a purely logical point of view I traced the road from Dhankuta northwards to Hille, a town which seemed to fulfil most of the criteria but somehow didn't feel right. So for a while I gave logic a miss; using my intuition, I was drawn to a part of the map showing a long valley running towards a mountain range, the Milke Danda, with a tributary of the River Arun on one side of a track and a ridge of hills on the other. At the lower end of the valley was a small town called Kokuwa, which had four tracks leading into it, the southern one leading eventually to Dhankuta, and a river loop near to it.

The valley itself was about 3–4 miles (5 km) wide and nearly 20 miles (32 km) long. Halfway along the valley on the track from Kokuwa was a small town named Chainpur, which I later heard mentioned as a Newar hill town. The Newars, I learned, are an ancient ethnic group forming three-quarters of the population of the capital, Kathmandu. Their architecture is of a pagoda style with overhanging eaves on the houses, and angled temple roofs. Their religion is a synthesis of Hinduism and Buddhism, which tied in very well with Nadia's experiences.

Three miles or so north-east along the track from Kokuwa was a peak which felt right for the hill behind Nadia's little village; the village itself would probably be too small to be marked on any map. The altitude of the valley was not noted, but the nearest peak whose height was indicated was 2777 m (9110 ft). Later I learned that at 2130 m (6990 ft) the climate makes the transition from subtropical to temperate, which would fit with the climatic conditions I expected.

At present the proper road only goes as far as Dhankuta, with an extension to Hille marked as asphalt-surfaced in parts. All points north are unsurfaced roads or tracks. The road I saw going through Nadia's village was still unsurfaced in fifty or sixty years' time, though carrying some traffic. The river was near enough to Kokuwa to be right; I had seen the men going out via the main through-road to work on the dam project. The main road would probably be the route from Dhankuta to Tumlingtar.

Going back to the map I had first drawn of Nadia's village (a copy of which I had sent to the publishers several months before acquiring the map of Nepal), I set about comparing my sketched layout with this valley, and checking whether any other valley might be similar enough to cause confusion. After very careful scrutiny I was certain that Kokuwa, as well as feeling intuitively right, was the only place on the large-scale map which had all the required features for the neighbouring town, including the roads and a loop of river. There was a very good chance that Kokowa was the town visited by Nadia.

I also wanted to check the information about Nepal and Nadia's life that I had seen both under hypnosis and over the preceding years, including the local birds, food, architecture, customs and so on. Looking through a dictionary hoping that it might give the distribution of mynah birds (which it didn't), I thought to look at 'dal' to see if it meant anything in English. It was given as 'a split grain, a common foodstuff in India', also spelt 'dhal' and 'daal'. How silly, I felt – what I had taken to be a road name might be nothing more than a café sign! Steve pointed out that it was possible that roads were not given names anyway, and after further research I found this indeed to be the case; very few Nepalese roads are named and the houses are not numbered. Later still I learned that 'daal' is the usual Nepali spelling; what 'mer' might mean was less certain.

Still pursuing reference books, I found that there are over eight hundred species of bird in Nepal, and that mynahs, as well as crows and magpies, tend to scavenge around areas where people live. There is also a jungle fowl that resembles a small, untidy chicken, which is pretty close to the bantam-like birds I had seen.

The forests and vegetation are more lush in eastern Nepal, where there is also heavier rainfall, tying in with my image of mud being washed down the hillsides. I also checked on local temperatures and found that they might be very comfortable, with no extremes of hot or cold.

I had described the tourists as American – in fact I had referred to anyone who was not Nepali or Indian as American. The Nepalese word for foreigner is *ideshi*, but I learned that many Nepalis today label all foreigners *Aamerikan*, regardless of their nationality. This means that people organising projects using local labour might not necessarily be American. At present most development work in Nepal is carried out by British companies, and this situation may well be the same in sixty years' time.

It also seems perfectly reasonable for the main project to be a hydroelectric scheme; some are already under way in Nepal, where the rainfall and mountainous terrain lend themselves to this kind of development. This one could be using a tributary of the River Arun; I discovered that there is a project under way on this river right now which has led to new road building in the area. So perhaps the road through Nadia's village will be completed fairly soon, if it is not already there.

I was surprised to find out how many of the towns already have an electricity supply. This led me back to my original concept of Nadia's village being in a backwater, since I was sure that it had no power. There was no sign of electrical appliances or even lighting, and in the evenings it was very dark indoors. There was a chance, however, that the town had electricity, particularly in the offices used by the development workers and in what I took to be a bank in the town centre.

Although I knew very little about Nepal before I embarked on all this research, I knew like most people that it is mountainous, and critics could accuse me of guessing that there would be hydroelectric projects under construction. However, when I saw and described the development under hypnosis it was without conscious control, and my attempts to describe what I saw used such vague terms as 'a wall to slow down the water' instead of 'dam'.

While I can't score many points for being right about Nepal

being mountainous, I was quite pleased at the results of some intensive investigation into the local soil types. I had mentioned a reddish, cohesive soil, which I had described as a sandy loam. It was one of the first things that struck me when I originally became aware of Nadia. I found, however, that the local rock types include granite and more commonly schist, gneiss, limestone and dolomite, none of which is red.

Trying to find an explanation for the reddish soil that I had seen led me into some in-depth research about geology and rock formations with the help of my stepfather, who has considerable knowledge of geology. I eventually found out that reddish soil could well exist in this region, being caused by iron deposits around granite intrusions. A geological map of the area, if one existed, could probably help to pinpoint the actual village. A drift-map would show the surface rock type and a stratigraphic map would show underlying faults, which would be helpful in locating iron deposits.

Much later, a television producer told me that red soil is quite common in parts of Nepal. She had made visits to the country, not unfortunately to any Newar hill towns, but to the north and west of this area. I showed her a sketch I had made of the temple, detailing the fleur-de-lys-style scrollwork at the roof edge, and was reassured when she told me it was a fairly typical local decoration.

Turning to more domestic matters, my reference to figs turned out to be appropriate. Every hill village has a *chautaara*, a sort of rest place with religious significance. It includes a platform flanked by two sacred trees, a *pipal* and a *bar*, both species of fig. Small monuments and shrines of the type I saw in the village and in the middle of the road in the town are called *chaitya*, and are commonplace all over Nepal.

The diet today consists mainly of lentil soup, rice and curried vegetables. I had mentioned several times eating a mixture of grains and pulses; this could be because Nepalese women usually finish off the scraps after their menfolk have eaten, by which time the food has probably been mixed together. There are several types of bread including chapati, a round, flat, unleavened loaf; Tibetan bread, which is also flat and round; and a potato pancake. Any of these could be the bread I described, though the Tibetan bread seems the most likely.

Buses in Nepal today – as in many developing countries – are often old and poorly maintained and run to no fixed timetable, much as I had described them, which suggests little improvement in the next fifty years or so! I had described the truck driver who collected surplus grain as Indian. I now found that many businesses are run by Indians, who are possibly more motivated than the Nepalis to work for financial gain.

As for camera equipment, I tried to find a brand that might account for the letters 'Nic' on the camera used to photograph Nadia and her friends. Only Nikon came close, but I had felt that the letters were in isolation rather than part of a word. I could find no other suitably named company that might eventually manufacture cameras.

I also investigated the religions of the area, and discovered that both Hinduism and Buddhism are practised in Nepal, as well as by the Newars who draw from both, and who are to be found in or close to the eastern Himalayan region where I had located Nadia's village. Indeed, as I had already discovered, the town near to where I felt the village was is described as a Newar hill town. This would account for the amulets hanging from shrines in the Hindu style, and for the fact that there seemed to be two types of holy men. I had said that the priests dressed in dark robes were more important to Nadia than those in light colours. Now I found that Buddhist monks wear maroon while Hindu priests wear saffron yellow.

The total sum of small but significant accuracies at last gave me hope that there was enough detail within my vision to have the confidence to tell others about it. I had never had any real doubt that I was seeing a future life that will become reality, but it was necessary to me to back this up as far as possible with fact.

Above all, though, it was the atmosphere, the quality of the life, that made the experience so totally real for me – far more than any objective details, important though these are. Since my first glimpse of that future existence I had been particularly intrigued by the strong differences in social attitudes between the Nepalese life and life in the West. The general attitude of fatalism, modesty and dignity of which I was so strongly aware is consistent with writings on contemporary Nepal.

In my present life I tend to be driven: if I have an idle moment, I soon find or make something to do. In Nadia's life, although there was a good deal of work, it was all done in a gentle, relaxed fashion. The busy-busy part of me no longer seemed to be there. This was partly due to the sense of belonging to an extended family, all of whose members shared the responsibilities; the people around were all content and well-adjusted. So, although Nadia's life will be short, I look forward to it almost as a holiday.

Life expectancy in Nepal is currently only fifty-four years for men and fifty-one for women. In most countries women live longer than men; Nepalese women may have a shorter lifespan because they do most of the heavy work and are always the last to eat. But as Nadia I had no sense of physical hardship. Even after ploughing through accounts of local diseases and health precautions recommended to tourists I still feel a sense of adventure and enthusiasm at the prospect of becoming part of such a radically different society, if only for a while. Any lifetime is very short, after all, and the things that really matter in the end are not necessarily material values, but our relationships and a simple joy in living.

Normally, although Jim guided me into the past, he would make absolutely no suggestions as to what I should see, and his questions were always open-ended. But there was one session when he decided to approach our experiment a little differently – and the results, too, were rather different.

After the touch on my shoulder Jim talked me down for longer than usual, asking me to imagine my body getting heavy, and to go deeply into the subconscious part of my mind. I felt as though I was floating in space, immobile in a timeless void, and completely at peace. Then Jim asked me to imagine stairs ahead of me. At the bottom of the stairs, he told me, I would see an infinitely long corridor lined with many, many doors; behind each door was a different memory stored in the subconscious at any point in time.

Step by step, counting from one to ten, I went down the stairs and saw the corridor, which was endless. As I began to move forwards past the first few doors, the air around me seemed to have a heavy texture. Jim instructed:

'Look for an interesting door, but don't stop at the first one, or even the second. Go on until there is a door that seems special.'

So I passed a red door which was the first to attract me, then a blue one, and moved on until I came to a golden-yellow door; light seemed to be spilling out from around the edges. This one I opened.

First there was just brilliant light. Then I saw a tree beneath which sat an old man with his head bowed in contemplation. As I began to recognise where I was, the tree now became pure light. I knew that I was in a between-life state. The man was an old friend; his name was Ram. Without speaking or gesturing, he welcomed me.

As I described to Jim what was going on, my voice slowed down, expressing the atmosphere of calm surrounding me. 'I know this place ... it's all right.'

'What is all right?'

'Everything, it's good, nothing matters now.'

'Have you been here before?'

'Many times . . . . Always.'

'Are you standing on the ground?'

'No.'

Bathed in the light and completely at peace, I allowed the joy to encompass me. This, I told Jim, was a healing place after life.

'Is this where you go between lives?'

'Yes.'

I would have been content to stay in that place for much longer, but Jim asked me to see the door. He instructed:

'Go back through the door now, and into the corridor. I want you to find a door which has a sad memory behind it.'

I found the door, but I didn't really want to open it. The

minute I was inside I knew where I was and what had happened. I was Nadia at about twenty-one, and in my arms I cradled the small, limp and lifeless body of a beautiful little girl, my daughter. I cried; the person in the hypnotist's chair had tears rolling down her cheeks, as Nadia and I cried together. There had been some sort of illness, I explained to Jim.

'And the doctor came?'

'No, no doctor came.'

The child was so beautiful; I hugged her and stroked her face.

'Do you have a belief, do you know that she will go somewhere where she will be happy?'

'Yes, I know this.'

I was taken back through the door.

As Nadia, I had described my first child as a daughter, while at a later age in the fields I had seen only a son. Though I had assumed that some children would have been left with a relative whilst Nadia was working in the fields, the loss of the daughter fitted this picture. I now wondered if this was why I kept seeing those same few moments in the house with the little girl in her cot. Perhaps because I could see this in my present, and presumably remember it in the future life as Nadia, even if only vaguely, this could explain the resignation I felt as Nadia, as though at some level she knew and accepted what was to follow.

The experience reminded me very much of another time under hypnosis when I became aware of the death of a child, during my life as Mary. Then I had recalled a baby boy who died at birth, and I knew that this was only about a year before Mary's death after childbirth. This whole episode I had only remembered with the aid of hypnosis, but it had later been confirmed as absolute fact. There was no reason to think that the future episode as Nadia with a dying child, also seen under hypnosis, was any less real. It felt equally real; the depth of emotion was the same, which is hardly surprising since as far as I am concerned we are all three the same person in different incarnations.

Although as Nadia I had held a dead child in my arms and felt the grief at this loss, curiously there seemed no lingering pain when I awoke from the hypnotised state. It was not that I was beginning to lack emotion, or even that I was shutting out things that I didn't want to face. It was something to do with a subtle change of attitude, which may in part have been connected with finding it easier to face difficulties if you have some expectation of what you will have to cope with.

But there was something else: this, I felt, was to do with my visit to the between-lives state. This state had been on my mind for a while before this session. I had been getting flashes of awareness of existence as being more than just life in a physical body. Now, remembering that incredible radiant light and the all-enveloping calm, I realised that all experience is transitory.

I had not consciously attributed this between-life vision to a particular point in time, but afterwards I realised that I had been experiencing the first moments after Nadia's death. There were two aspects of the experience which would be particularly meaningful to Nadia. Firstly, Buddha sat under a tree when he attained enlightenment; secondly, Ram is the name given to the mortal form of Vishnu ('the one who works everywhere'), one of the gods of the Hindu trinity. This combination of Buddhist and Hindu symbolism would be in keeping with Nadia's religion.

I cannot prove that I will live as Nadia in the middle of the next century. My own certainty is based partly on the fact that much of what I have seen and remembered under hypnosis or in dreams or visions has turned out to be accurate, and partly on the emotional quality of the experience. I have to accept that many of the details cannot be confirmed until Nadia comes into physical existence, but I also have to accept that Nadia is my future. I feel that one day in the 2050s a visitor will come to the eastern Himalayas, who will be passing through a village where an insignificant girl called Nadia lives, and who will take a photograph of her and her sisters laughing in the sunshine beside the largest field.

CHAPTER 10

Future Living

Life in the twenty-third century

Over the years, and particularly as a teenager, I had had a number of brief visions of the distant future. Usually these were fragmentary images seen in almost subliminal flashes that left me with a feeling rather than a complete picture. Some were connected with my family; on one occasion I saw my grandchildren. But most were quite unconnected and difficult to place in time. Because these visions were often confusing, it was hard to pick out details that might be useful. However, I somehow knew that they belonged to the distant future, and the one consistent feature that gave me a real cause for concern was the lack of population, both human and animal.

The most vivid and long-lasting of these visions was on the occasion when I saw the past and future in connection with Peter Harris's cottage. Because so much of what I had seen then had already come about, there was a good chance that the rest of the vision was also accurate, including the lack of population. It was after this that my other future flashes began to fall into place like pieces of a jigsaw. This heightened my interest in exploring the distant future, and perhaps finding a possible explanation for the curiously empty world.

Because most of my future visions apart from Nadia had been of the Western world, the drop in population could be a Western phenomenon. Considering this, I felt it might be associated with our lifestyle – for example with the effects of artificial additives in food production. It could also be due to deliberate population control, but this would not account for the reduction in animal numbers. It seemed much more likely that more widespread environmental factors were responsible.

During my visits to Nadia's life under hypnosis Jim would move my consciousness about in time, and small scenes would come up that seemed connected with other possible future lives. Using progression hypnosis, it was almost inevitable that not everything I saw would be confined to the future in Nepal. I was very aware that precognition and progression should not be accepted as an actual future without some strong evidence, but I was intrigued by the details that slowly emerged.

During my very last hypnosis session Jim took me through a kind of summing-up process, bouncing me through all the time periods I had visited in previous sessions, both past and future, to check whether they were consistent. He also asked me to look at a period beyond the end of Nadia's life, and here I was given a very brief glimpse of a fairly distressing event. The time was somewhere around 2150 and I was in mainland Europe, possibly Poland.

I was cradling my husband's head and comforting him as he died, probably of natural causes but aged only about fifty. There were signs of poverty and hardship in our clothes and demeanour, and a sense of stress and resignation that went beyond the natural grief of the moment. We did not seem to be in a wartime situation, but it was clear that life was hard. The only positive feelings were the will to survive and my love for my husband, whom I felt was the same person as my present-day husband. This was the worst period I had seen in any of my future visions, with or without hypnosis, and I have the sense that this may be a generally low point – perhaps the lowest – in our future history. The lives that were to come after it were much more positive.

When Jim asked me to explore the corridor with its infinity of doors, I came to one or two that had no connection with Nadia's life. It was behind one of these doors that I found the scene with Gwen, the twelfth-century young woman described in Chapter 4. Another door that I was drawn to was made of textured wood, and I opened it to find myself touching the thick and fissured bark of a huge tree. My first comment was about the thickness and sponginess of the bark.

I was a dumpy, single woman; I gave my age as 'the wrong side of thirty' and my name, tentatively as always, as Janice Thorpe. I was studying the tree, and making notes on it.

'What is the date?'

Unhelpfully I replied, 'The 16th.' Then, after more prompting, 'June.' Asked the year, I said, ''28,' and then at last, '2228.'

The fact was that I wasn't really interested in talking or answering questions – I had work to do. My job was to take a core sample of this beautiful giant tree, which would be passed to someone else to study for its possible medical or other uses. 'There might even be textile uses,' I told Jim, 'because this bark is really quite fibrous. It's like a cork, but not a true cork.'

I went ahead and took a minute sample, using a syringe-type tool. I then carefully packed the sample into a numbered container, and then in a squarish field-bag which I labelled. I was doing field-work in South America, with some other people. We were staying in tents, to keep costs down. We had to be a bit careful of insects, but there were no big animals left in the area.

I was short and plump, dressed in a slightly tailored, almost safari-style jacket and short skirt which was none too comfortable around the ampler areas of my anatomy. It wasn't a uniform but, somewhat incongruously, worn by choice. My shoes were flat and comfortable, but of a soft fabric which was not really practical for off-road walking. The field-bag I carried was covered in a military green fabric. It seemed that this was a city girl's idea of what to wear on an expedition.

I enjoyed this part of my job; back home I did lab-work. I

described myself as having had a standard education; I was a technician, my job was 'not special'. My office base was in Jersey, USA; the company I was working for was Unichem. This was about the furthest I had travelled for them.

'Did they fly you in?' asked Jim.

'They couldn't. We had to come by truck, a heck of a way, from a port in Brazil.' I had a vague impression of travelling by ship, on an ordinary passenger route.

Jim asked about the roads and whether there was much vegetation, since at one time they had been destroying quite a lot of the forest.

'They can't touch this patch,' I told him. If we found a use for the trees, there would be long-term forest farming. The tree I was looking at was very old; they wouldn't take old trees but would use seeds and young trees if the chemical structure was right. Synthetic chemicals could be produced but were not as good, because of their by-products.

The fuel powering the truck was a kind of fermented spirit. Some countries still used petrol, but 'it's not a good idea.' Back home there were very strict rules about transportation. Private transport was restricted, which didn't seem to bother me. I lived not far from the industrial area where I usually worked, and didn't travel much, though I was going to spend my holiday with my parents, who lived a little way away; I was very attached to them.

My home was included as part of my salary. I could see the area where I lived, which was fairly unattractive and quite similar to the older areas of any inner city today. This was my only future vision in which the population decline was not obvious, although there were a number of empty buildings.

Jim asked whether there was much crime – did people get murdered or robbed, as happens in crowded inner cities?

'No, no.' I sounded slightly surprised. Questioned further, I said, 'It's not crowded.'

I didn't know what the population figures were, though I thought it was fairly stable. Most of the American population lived along the coasts, while the middle was fairly empty.

Most people worked; there was a lot of work to be done, I said. In my leisure time, the indoor shopping mall near my home area was a favourite place for me, full of noise and activity. I was able to see and describe it. It didn't seem especially crowded, and was built over a large area and on several levels. I liked to window-shop, 'looking at the screens'. The advertisements that filled every available space were moving or video rather than static pictures; they supplemented and frequently replaced window displays, so there was no need to walk around the shops.

Other details were consistent with my previous visions of the future. The air was clean, Janice reported, but the sea was polluted and could not be used as a source of food. Nobody was allowed to pump anything into the oceans any more, but over the years there had been a general toxic build-up that had spread through all the oceans, as water-soluble chemical which would take a long time to break down had been carried out from the land.

Jim asked whether I knew what was the most important scientific discovery or invention over the last hundred years. All that came to my mind was a beam of light used for diagnosis in hospitals and laboratory analysis, apparently an extension of laser technology. It seemed to work by taking measurements of the interruptions to light as the beam passed through living tissues, showing up abnormalities due to frequency changes. The beam was also used on core samples from plants, as the first stage of analysis. Also in the field of medicine, there was a sonic treatment for breaking down blood clots, though 'if you are monitored you shouldn't have blood clots.' Average life expectancy, Janice thought, was around the mid-eighties.

'What about cancer?'

'That's a pollution disease, isn't it? You can treat it – it's just unpleasant. It's caused by anything that disrupts the normal function of the cell.'

Asked further about pollution, Janice said the air was OK. 'Plants are pretty good at cleaning the air if you let them get on with it. The air's not a big problem – it's mostly in water and in the food-chain.'

Two months after this session I came across a reference to cancer studies in Britain and America which concluded that, despite the advances in medicine, there has been a steady increase in cancer deaths over the last thirty years.

The next life chronologically was that of another American, Sheryl Vaughn. She actually came up in our sessions before Janice, and we returned to her more than once. At our first encounter she was a slight, blonde, fifteen-year-old schoolgirl living in California in the year 2285. It seemed to be a time full of hope and enthusiasm.

On entering the hypnotic state I immediately found myself in a classroom, in a study group with about twenty-five other students of mixed ages. We were discussing ideas about time and physics, and how all subjects were interlinked. 'It's about how to understand how time affects us, how we use time to understand other ideas,' I told Jim. 'It's quite complex – it's not my best subject.'

My first answers came with many pauses; I didn't want to be interrupted by questions but to listen to what the teacher was saying. The class interaction was good, with enthusiastic questions and answers from most of the students. It was as though we were all there because we wanted to gain from the experience of learning rather than because we had to be there. We didn't take exams, but had assessments to decide whether we would go on for further education, and where we would be usefully employed.

The class structure seemed to be traditional, with the teacher standing at the front and a screen for displaying written and pictorial material. We also learned by listening to recordings. 'Listening is the best way to learn,' I said.

Jim asked whether this was done subliminally.

'It doesn't last long enough when it's done like that. The important thing is understanding, so you can think, using the ideas. You don't need to learn everything if you can find the information.'

We used computers too; the most important was linked to a

network. 'But they won't join it all up. There's a risk with too large a network of people controlling the information, so they're in small networks.' We had a computer at home that linked up with others.

When Jim asked me about my home, I commented that a lot of places had been left empty. I lived with my mother, though my father was still around.

'How long do people live, on average?'

'It depends. The trouble is if you get too old you get lots of problems. It's not worth going on – no more than eighty. But some live to over a hundred.'

Jim decided to revisit Sheryl more than once. At the next session he asked me to go to her at the age of twenty-five. I found myself walking from my home to a park, down a fairly steep road. It was a sunny day and I was wearing a white, short-sleeved loose shirt, possibly with shorts, and felt comfortable. I seemed to be wearing something on my left wrist. (In the present I wear no watch or bracelets, so I was aware of the difference.) The air was clean and the sun bright, just as it had been in my vision at the junk shop.

There were other similarities to my previous visions of the future. Some buildings stood empty, which, combined with my earlier impression of small classes with pupils of different ages, suggested that only a few families lived in the area. What was particularly striking was a sense of safety and security. I had the feeling that I could happily leave my house with the front door unlocked.

Jim asked about my work, and I told him I worked from home using a console linked to agency computers. I lived alone and was not particularly interested in getting married, but I had friends in the area and we used to visit each other to share meals. I could see my home, a single-storey building that opened straight on to the street. The main room felt airy, and was decorated in a simple style in pale pastel shades; most of the furnishing was white. It seemed to be a multi-purpose, open-plan room, and the pale colours and careful lighting and design gave an illusion of greater space than may have been there. It seemed like a living area designed for one person, with only a few adjoining rooms.

The computer console sat against one wall, which was filled with shelves containing files, many with paper documents, and removable items whose purpose I was unable to determine. This part of the room was basically a work station with a desk section in the middle, and everything else arranged each side, floor to ceiling. The room also contained what looked like a breakfast bar attached to a kitchen area, and a table-height work surface jutting into the room space.

Jim asked me what my job was about. I said that it was to do with the living sciences, to do with plants and animals and the interdependent relationships between living things. Pushed for further explanations, I continued to talk at some length. In this persona, I felt full of energy and found it fairly easy to talk. I explained that companies would go to the agency I worked for, to find out what the best crops would be for replanting a particular area. This could be anywhere in the world and involved someone taking soil samples and assessing the local plant diseases and pests. Insect pests were not considered too much of a problem as they could be controlled with the use of predators, usually other insects, but the whole environmental balance had to be carefully calculated. The biggest problem was fungal attack, to which organisms are vulnerable under stress or when immunity is depleted.

My job was to collate all the available information and present a package listing resistant plant strains that would not upset the balance of the location in question. The list would include groups of crop plants and trees; under certain circumstances there might be a recommendation to reforest rather than grow crops. We had to take into consideration a variety of environmental needs specific to the area and climate. My list would then be added to reports by other workers giving information on aspects such as pest control methods, which were usually biological.

The purpose of all this was both economic and environmental, I told Jim; it was much better to balance things up naturally without using chemicals. The worst form of pollution was still chemical. Although the situation was improving, chemical farming methods were considered extremely dangerous as most soils were still heavily damaged by excessive chemical usage in the past, which had also affected water supplies.

Although I talked about the complexity of the job with some authority, my personal place in the organisation was not especially prestigious; my job was mainly clerical. However, it required an understanding of the material I had to collate, and I enjoyed my work. It gave me the sense of doing something worthwhile.

Jim next asked me about sources of energy. I answered that we used solar energy and other renewable sources. We didn't like to burn coal, oil or other fuels. There were still some problems with oil pollution, though we used bacteria to consume the oil.

Jim asked me more about pollution – when had it reached its peak? I named two periods of high pollution, one at the beginning of the Industrial Revolution, mainly caused by burning fuels and atmospheric pollution, and the later era (coinciding with our present times) when chemical pollution was the main problem. There were also difficulties with the atmosphere at that period, but they were relatively easy to correct in time. The chemicals, however, had stayed in the soil and eventually contaminated the water.

During the phase of chemical pollution, the birds had been the first to suffer. I was not completely sure why, but I knew that one reason was that the change in the atmosphere had encouraged different organisms to breed which had affected the birds, although they still survived in some areas. Marine animals had the worst problem, because their environment was still heavily polluted. However, despite an increased likelihood of disease from chemically altered bacteria, they were still holding out, including a few species of whale. Although the seas were polluted, it was easier to protect them there than to try to keep them in sanctuaries.

All the animals, including people, had suffered some damage from the cocktail of chemicals. The main problem seemed to be infertility. There were fewer animals of all types including humankind, and there had been a considerable drop in the human population. This had been a good thing at first, but it was worrying that the chemicals were still affecting fertility.

Not long after this I came across a reference to the work of Dr Helen Wambach and Dr Chet Snow: a pilot study into future life progression called *Mass Dreams of the Future*. Eleven hundred hypnotised subjects had been asked to go forward to the years 2100 and 2300. Eighty-nine of the volunteers managed to see themselves in a possible life during one or both of these years.

From my own point of view the most interesting aspect of the research was that the study suggested a 95 per cent drop in population by the year 2100. Only about 5 per cent of the volunteers saw themselves in a life in 2100, and 12 per cent in 2300.

The participants fell into four types: those who saw themselves living in space or on other planets; those in New Age-style communities isolated from society; those in artificial enclosed or underground cities; and those in simple, rural survivalist groups with no modern technology. Few, if any, described a lifestyle whose structure had any continuity with the present. Hypnotic progression is problematic, even under carefully controlled conditions. These people were hypnotised *en masse* as a group, and I can't help wondering whether their visions were influenced by science fiction, or by their own expectations and imaginations.

This possibility was something I was constantly taking into account in my own sessions. When released from the hypnotic trance after this last session with Sheryl, I felt it necessary to talk to Jim about its similarities to what I had already seen in my other glimpses of the future. Sheryl had spoken of a reduction in the population, in the Western world particularly, and a loss of animal numbers, especially birds, although the air was clean. It was possible that I could have been imposing on Sheryl's future my presuppositions gained from my other future visions.

There was one difference, however. One of my assumptions had been that a major cause of problems would be an increase in sunlight, due to damage to the ozone layer. But Sheryl had pretty well dismissed this idea. It could be that the problem will be solved by the reduction in pollution, including traffic pollution, and assisted by the reduction in human numbers.

The only other point of significance was that, throughout the time under hypnosis when I was speaking as Sheryl, I was shivering – which is something that often happens to me when seeing the future using psychometry. This stopped when I came out of hypnosis.

I made sure that the timespans for my two future personalities would fit in with each other. Janice had given an age of over thirty in 2228, and Sheryl was fifteen in 2285. This would give Janice a lifespan of about seventy-two – more if she was well over thirty. So there could be a reasonable gap between lives. It was encouraging to find that these two personalities could run one after the other so comfortably.

It was interesting that both personalities had an interest in ecological science and worked in botanical research, though Janice had a less qualified role. This suggested both a continuity and a development of interests and skills, which supports the idea that people can bring into a new life skills already learned from a previous one. One of my own main areas of interest has been biology, particularly human physiology, but I can easily envisage developing a germ of interest in plants, particularly over several lifetimes.

The two accounts included consistencies in the descriptions of the environmental and population changes. Some of the scientific aspects could prove interesting, though I hadn't the background to know if they were viable. They included the use of fermented fuel for vehicles, which would be clean and renewable, unlike oil-based products, and the light beam that could be used for tissue analysis – a process which could rely on some form of spectrum analysis.

A good while later, I was able to find out more about current trials of alternative sources of fuel. For instance, I read that the engineers at Rover are working on a fuel derived from oilseed rape, which they hope will power an unmodified diesel engine. Media coverage has been given to other experiments, including methane derived from chicken manure used to power trucks.

And there has been work on the commercial production of electric cars for a very long time, though I have not seen these yet in any of my future-time glimpses. I also recently read that the Brazilians are now fermenting sugar to produce an alcohol which is used for fuel – when I came across this item I wondered whether the comments I had made under hypnosis should be classified as coincidence, telepathy or precognition!

I could also have been using my present-day knowledge when I was asked about space exploration. Jim asked both Janice and Sheryl about advances in space, and it seems there is a long way to go before real life catches up with science fiction. Janice had commented that most research was with unmanned probes and that a study of the planets of the solar system was being undertaken, including trying to develop an ecology on Mars, which would be a very long process. Exploration outside the solar system she described as almost non-existent. Sheryl said that the human colonisation of space was still a very long way off, but there was some research into finding micro-organisms in space, which demanded great care in handling because of their unknown effects.

Here I could in part have been echoing what I already knew: there are already projects under way looking into the possibilities of developing Mars, trying to grow things there and create an atmosphere. From my own experience, I had no doubt that precognition can be reliable, but I still had difficulty in assessing the value of hypnotically retrieved information. Should it all be judged on the same footing? My past-life memories as Mary had definitely been helped by the hypnosis, even though at the time I felt very unsure about the accuracy of the information I was retrieving. I was quite certain that I had seen my future life as Nadia because the hypnosis revealed places and events that matched my spontaneous visions.

I realised that there were only two ways to find out whether precognition of the distant future had a chance of being right. One was to look back at other, earlier insights for their accuracy; this was not a problem. The other was to look at present trends to see whether any of them might already be leading us towards the envisaged future. What I was not aware of at that stage was the wealth of information available about changes to the environment, and consequently to our health, that could point the way towards just the sort of future that I had seen.

CHAPTER 11

Our Planetary Future

The population in decline

Today, one of the planet's major problems is over-population. Yet my visions of the future showed a severe drop in the numbers of both people and animals, although plant life seemed to be flourishing. There was no evidence of any major disaster, and during my drift in time towards this future I had not seen or sensed anything unusually dangerous. But a particular problem mentioned by both Janice and Sheryl was chemical pollution.

After my vision of the English Midlands two hundred years ahead I was so puzzled by the lack of people that I decided then to keep my eye open for any research that might shed light on its causes. The first piece of evidence that came my way was a scientific paper giving details of a periodic test on students at an American university. When it was first mentioned in newspaper items in the early 1980s it caused little more than a ripple of reaction, but to me it was fascinating. During routine sperm motility tests on students in their early twenties, it was found that there had been a drop in fertility since the previous test at the same university ten years earlier. The drop was not great, but over such a short timespan it was significant. At the time, no reasons for this were suggested.

Then, during the hot dry summers of the mid-1980s, tests on the amount of pollutants dissolved in the reduced water reserves in London showed that the greatest source of pollution consisted of chemicals that acted like female hormones. At first it was thought that these must originate entirely from contraceptive drugs. Since the Pill had been with us since the 1960s, some of the hormones would have found their way via sewage into drinking water supplies and might not be being broken down fast enough by natural processes to disperse effectively. Men exposed to female hormones could be expected to suffer reduced fertility, so the item was of considerable interest. A pollutant in the drinking water that led to infertility could be an obvious cause for an eventual reduction in the population of both people and animals.

Female hormones, among numerous other drugs, have also been used by the food industry. Although these are no longer used to produce capons (male chickens made plump by the use of female hormones), all types of food production use other drugs that may be just as damaging to fertility, as well as reducing resistance to disease. No one really knows their long-term effects. Anything that enters the body as a fat-soluble substance may remain stored in our fat reserves for ten or twenty years, probably even longer, and new drugs or food additives are simply not tested over such extensive periods.

Towards the end of 1992 new information revealed a much more dramatic and widespread loss in fertility. In the Western world sperm counts were shown to have dropped by 50 per cent over a fifty-year period by Professor Niels Skakkebaek at Copenhagen University, who between 1938 and 1991 carried out a series of 61 studies involving 14,947 men. Following further tests in Britain which confirmed these results, reports stated that one in twenty men was believed to be infertile. Today a normal sperm count is expected to be only one-third of the average figure when tests first started in the 1930s.

According to news reports, the culprits responsible for this sperm reduction were believed to be environmental toxins and pollutants, together with an increase in living in over-heated environments. The question of the exposure to female hormones, or to chemicals mimicking the action of such hormones, was not at first mentioned.

There were other possible contributing factors not cited, such as radiation. There has been a steady increase in background radiation, due in part to the normal use of hospital X-ray equipment (the risk of radiation release is a problem admitted by radiotherapists) and also by residue from atomic bomb tests carried out during and since the 1960s, often in secret.

All of these factors could easily affect animal fertility as well as human. My vision of the future was beginning to make sense.

A further reference to infertility was made, among others, in a brief reply to a student's question published in the *Daily Telegraph* on 30 August 1993. Dr Richard Sharpe of the Medical Research Council's Reproductive Biology Unit in Edinburgh suggested more than one possible cause for the drop in fertility. One was that the process of sperm production was impaired by exposure to heat, radiation and chemicals. The other was that the development in early life of the Sertoli cells, responsible for sperm production, could be affected by toxins in our food and water, which mimic the effects of the female sex hormone oestrogen. These toxins include pesticides, dioxins (used in bleaching paper and other products) and PCBs (polychlorinated biphenyls, industrial pollutants from electrical equipment). This came much closer to describing the causes that I had begun to suspect. As scientists now began to discuss the problem, further information became available.

Exposure to PCBs and possibly other chemicals during pregnancy is also thought to affect the male foetus, giving rise to fertility problems in later life, and sometimes to abnormalities of the male genitalia. They may also be passed on in breast-feeding, since human milk is high in fat. This means that chemicals in the food chain not only enter our own bodies, where they can be stored, but can affect our children's ability to reproduce.

Some plastics have also been found to leach chemicals that

mimic female hormones. Since these chemicals do not break down naturally, the quantity entering the food chain, and subsequently our bodies, is constantly accumulating. This would create an ongoing effect through the generations, leading to a widespread increase in infertility that would eventually result in a drop in population. As I write in 1995, the annual fall in male fertility of up to 2.6 per cent is becoming a problem of international concern; experts are now studying the effects of possible oestrogen-mimicking chemicals in approximately four hundred mainly man-made substances, ranging from pesticides to paint additives, the suspect being an industrial detergent called nonylphenol (*Sunday Times*, 21 May 1995; *The Times*, 7 June 1995).

It is not only human fertility that is at risk; a problem has been occurring with a large number of fish in British rivers. Female hormones and oestrogen-mimicking chemicals, entering our water via sewage outlets, have so badly affected the fish that many are unable to breed. Dr Paul Johnson of Greenpeace has expressed his concern over fish populations and the health of our rivers. In fact, hermaphrodite fish (infertile 'feminised' male fish) were found in the River Lea in Welwyn Garden City in Hertfordshire as long ago as 1978. And a year before that experiments were carried out using hormones on young male trout which resulted in their producing female egg proteins, thus proving that hormones could adversely affect the breeding ability of fish.

As I read the increasing amount of evidence over the years, it became clear that a future I had seen as unlikely and puzzling in the 1980s is more and more likely to come about. In fact, a study published on 11 July 1994 (World Population Day) shows that the increase in population that the world has been experiencing until now is in decline and could be going into reverse. At the current rate, by the year 2100 the population could be back to 1980 levels (*Reincarnation International*, Issue 3). However, based on the drastic reduction I have seen within two hundred years, I believe that the fall in population will pick up speed and will happen much faster than this.

Of course, it is not only fertility that is affected by chemical pollution; human and animal immune systems are also at risk. We have now reached a point where our pollution of the sea is destroying the immunity of large marine animals, so that they are suffering and dying from diseases to which they normally have resistance. The fat-soluble chemicals have been a concern of mine since my college days over twenty years ago, when their effects on the whale population began to be drawn to our attention. This problem was mentioned in 1993 in wildlife television programmes which expressed a concern for the whales which are being attacked by serious disease all over the world. It is believed that their immunity has been affected by a build-up of toxins in their body fats which are passed on to the young through the mothers' milk. A few years ago the seal population began to suffer in a very similar way, dying in their thousands. All of this suggests that we too may eventually be damaged by these toxins and less able to fight common diseases.

An article in the *Observer* of 13 March 1994 examined the problems of PCBs and other pollutants in the North Sea which are 'killing the sea'. The oxygen content of the water is dropping, killing fish, and some pollutants are poisoning them directly. Fishermen have commented on the bizarre deformities now being found in an increasing percentage of their catch: grotesque fish with major physical abnormalities and cancerous growths.

Further problems too have been attributed to poisons in the sea and fat-soluble pollutants. Between 1988 and 1993 a number of children in coastal areas were born with birth defects to the hands. This kind of defect occurs spontaneously from time to time, but the number and the clustered locations of these cases seemed significant. In an article discussing the incidence and possible causes of this defect Dr Alister Hay, a senior lecturer in chemical pathology at Leeds University, commented that PCBs, dioxins and banned pesticides such as DDT were widely present in fatty human tissue (*Sunday Times*, 23 January 1994). On land, too, fungicides and pesticides have been suspected of causing clusters of children born with tiny eyes or none at all (*Observer*, 30 May 1993).

From all of this I think we may assume that fat-soluble pollutants are already in our bodies and a sequence of events is already in motion. We are now heading towards a future where we carry with us the long-term effects of pollution, and it will take a number of generations before it will be possible to reduce the level of toxins in human and animal bodies. Meanwhile, our immune systems and therefore our general health are already being affected.

In several of my distant-future sessions under hypnosis cancer was mentioned as the major medical problem, though treatable; it is already known to be on the increase. Current cancer research suggests that there are inherited factors that put people in a high-risk category, and perhaps these could eventually be tackled genetically. But from what I have seen, I believe it will still be an uphill battle as other areas of risk threaten our immune systems.

Another cause for a fall in human numbers, and one which would explain the speed at which I believe it will occur, could be the sudden appearance of a number of new viruses, for example the HIV virus responsible for Acquired Immunity Disorder Syndrome (AIDS) which emerged during the 1980s. It appears to have started in Africa, one of the areas badly affected by radiation from atomic bomb tests at sea, due to the prevailing winds and tides. During the 1970s a number of newspaper articles in African countries expressed considerable concern about the concentration of fall-out, particularly over Central Africa. Nobody knew what the effects of the radiation would mean to that continent, but the effects of the HIV virus have reached most of the rest of the world. Radiation at normal levels is responsible for changes in evolution. It is not at all inconceivable that higher than usual levels of radioactivity should cause a more rapid development within small organisms such as viruses and bacteria at the same time as reducing people's immunity.

Other new viruses include a small but increasing number of childhood diseases. When my own children contracted 'hand, foot and mouth', a virus infection which causes vesicles on these areas (and has nothing to do with foot and mouth disease in animals) I was assured that this was a normal childhood disease, yet it did not to my knowledge exist in my own childhood. A variety of 'mimic' illnesses have also arisen which have similarities to rubella and glandular fever, to mention but two. And, just to confuse the situation further, the over-use of antibiotics has led to many quite lethal viruses and bacteria developing new and more virulent strains. One of these is the virus responsible for tuberculosis, a problem which was thought to have been beaten but is once more on the increase. It is interesting that by the 1970s the American astrologer Al Morrison had forecast a mutation of bacteria and viruses for the period between 1984 and 1995 (Joe Fisher, *The Case for Reincarnation*).

Rapid mutation due to radiation is liable to affect simple organisms first, so bacterial and viral evolution was to be expected. The next stage would be for some plants and then insects to change. I keep my eyes open for new varieties of insects in particular, as plants are often subject to man's direct interference. But a rapid and varied, spontaneous alteration in wild plant species has been observed close to atomic power stations.

Also linked to pollution, as well as to food additives, is the increased occurrence of allergies. There has been a huge increase in childhood asthma, which has been linked with the by-products of vehicle exhaust fumes. Although many allergies are looked upon as a mere inconvenience, some are extremely dangerous. Asthma can kill; so can anaphylaxsis, an extreme allergic reaction to anything from antibiotics to food colouring. These allergies can start at any time of life without warning.

There are several theories as to why people may suddenly develop an allergy or, increasingly these days, multiple allergy syndrome which causes the body to react to a whole range of substances. One suggested explanation is that the number of chemicals that our bodies now have to cope with causes a breakdown of the normal immune response. Even everyday products like washing powder, soaps and shampoos contain many ingredients known to cause allergies in some people, adding to the general bombardment of foreign substances that we have to cope with. Most of these substances have only been developed in the second half of this century, so we have no idea of their long-term effects.

Another cause of damage to our immune systems is the increase in unscreened light, due to the thinning of the protective ozone layer. This may be one of the main reasons for the sudden deaths, over the last few years, of a large percentage of the frog and toad population all over the world. In parts of Canada, over which the ozone depletion is fairly extensive, up to 95 per cent of frog eggs now fail to hatch, while of those that do many are undersized or fail to mature. Amphibians have particularly sensitive skin which reacts to the increased sunlight, but their situation only reflects the problems that all life forms on this planet will have to learn to contend with if they are to survive. As the thinner ozone layer allows more unscreened light through, damage to our immune systems would mean that diseases generally will also increase, including not only skin cancer but all types of cancer.

Even if medicine continues to improve, medical advances in themselves could weaken the gene pool. As people with hereditary illnesses, such as diabetes, survive for longer, there is a possibility that more children will be produced carrying inherited diseases. As time goes on, medical advances could therefore result in a larger proportion of the population being less healthy and less able to fight off ordinary illnesses. The resultant stress on the general population could be another factor in population reduction. The only hope is that medicine may develop ways to cure the problem at the level of the risk-carrying genes, through genetic engineering.

Of course, a reduction in population in itself does not currently appear disastrous. There is no doubt that there are now too many people in the world to live in reasonable comfort. Not only is it harder to feed more people without using potentially damaging chemical farming methods, but overcrowded conditions lead to social problems. Rats will kill each other if kept in overcrowded cages, and some farm animals are known to become aggressive if confined with others in small spaces. At the human level, over-population leads to poverty, hunger and an increase in violence of all kinds.

Whenever the world became overpopulated in the past, the numbers were cut down again by famine and the diseases of overpopulation such as bubonic plague, cholera and typhus; or there were mass migrations of people to less crowded regions of the world. But we have adapted the way we live to allow more people to be sustained on the same land than has ever been possible before. And alongside the very advances that have enabled this increase in population, the levels of pollution and pollution-related diseases go up as the numbers of machines, cars and factories increase to meet the needs of the extra people.

What can be done to restore health to the planet? I have already mentioned the Gaia theory, the idea that the planet is a self-regulating system, capable of restoring its own balance. The balance of nature has been understood in general terms for a long time. We know that if one creature is removed from the food chain its predators suffer and die, and its food sources multiply to excess. The Gaia theory takes this process further, including even the very controlled balance of gases in our atmosphere. For example, if there was a fraction too little oxygen in our air, animals would be unable to breathe; if there were too much, there would be a constant risk of fire by spontaneous combustion. Somehow this delicate balance continues to be maintained.

The theory is that this system is not accidental, but controlled. The so-called greenhouse gases that we produce in abundance are broken down by nature in order to maintain that essential balance, in much the same way that it would break down gases produced by natural means.

Of course, it is not enough for us to sit back and trust nature to work fast enough to heal all the wounds that we so rapidly create. Indeed, if we left all the problems of pollution for nature to solve we might just have to accept our own demise as a part of the solution. Fortunately, scientists and others are beginning to look at ways in which we can cooperate with nature.

For example, scientists have recently taken an interest in a giant mat of algae that grew in a particular area of the ocean in prehistoric times. It is normal for algae to grow seasonally in the ocean; it was the quantity and area of this growth that gave rise to particular interest. Its purpose was apparently to trap an excess of free carbon dioxide, possibly due to volcanic activity, which was causing an atmospheric imbalance. The algae would absorb and trap the gas, then die and sink to the ocean floor. During the last Ice Age the bloom of algae grew as far south as the Canaries; now algae are normally limited to a smaller area mainly restricted to the northern hemisphere. Then in 1993 a huge and growing mat of algae was found in the same part of the ocean that had been covered by the prehistoric growth – at a time when we realised that we were producing too much carbon dioxide and upsetting the balance of gases in our atmosphere, possibly giving rise to the greenhouse effect.

This time, man is taking a hand in restoring the balance. Some large companies such as Shell are now funding research into algae growth so as to speed up the natural process and thus combat global warming. This work is mainly being carried out in the southern hemisphere, where there are fewer algae, by adding iron to the ocean. So far there has not been a noticeable increase in uptake of excess carbon dioxide, but the research continues and may yet produce results.

From what I have seen of the future, this points the way towards other means by which we can actively participate in Gaia's self-regulation of the environment. Although we have created a difficult situation for ourselves on this planet, the future I saw was full of hope. There would be fewer people, who would be combining a sensible control of the environment with a greater understanding of their responsibility for the wellbeing of the whole. Although I did not see what was happening in the rest of the world, Sheryl's work in America seemed to involve international cooperation, at least in the world of ecology and food production, and there was little sense of national borders. Could it be that we will be expending our intelligence and resources on environmental care rather than on warfare and competition between nations?

I did not see us going back to a simpler, less technological life; rather, we will be using a greater degree of technology which will be in harmony with the environment: It may not be a perfect existence, but the air will be clean and the crops healthy. What I do see is a chance for us to live a better life.

Each time Jim progressed me to the distant future he asked whether there was violence or danger in the society. Each time I answered that there was not, in a tone expressing surprise at being asked such a question. Indeed, I was very struck by the sense of security in Sheryl's life. A reduction in crime and violence could be one of the very beneficial results of reduced population. Overcrowding and poverty should be eradicated, and there will be employment for everyone. At the same time, a much lower birth rate will mean that children are really wanted and valued, and improvements in our approach to their needs, development and education will help to produce fewer maladjusted individuals.

Some people believe that if visions of the future are right, and show that everything will work out in our favour, there is no need to worry about what we are doing now. Others with equal fatalism feel that we can have no power to change the course of events. But we do have free will, and humanity is possibly more capable of influencing future environmental conditions than any other single factor. It is not reasonable to abdicate responsibility for the future. What we do intentionally to improve and protect the environment today is a vital part of the complex picture that makes tomorrow.

CHAPTER 12

The Magic Garden

Creating tomorrow

A single lifespan is so brief that we have little time to begin to understand ourselves or others, to find a purpose or a sense of fulfilment. Yet our perspective of time can reach into history and our own past lives, touch that magical, tranquil state between lives, and experience the promise of other lives to come. This sense of continuity can take us beyond the confines of one life and beyond the isolation of the individual.

It is not necessary to have recall of past lives to understand and accept their reality, and to have a sense of the continuity of the soul. Nor is it essential to have a near-death experience to appreciate that life continues after we leave the body or to trust in the promise of tremendous peace and happiness in that other existence. We do not have to have psychic visions of the future in order to have hope for the tomorrow of our species.

I do not expect everyone to accept my visions as real, but just to consider their possibilities can cast a whole different light on the life that we are living today. My aim is not necessarily to change people's beliefs, but perhaps to open their minds to other options, and to the idea that a better future is possible for humanity and the planet. Those who believe that we live once only may not care what the world is like in two hundred years' time. If we live many lifetimes, then the picture changes radically. We will continue to live with the consequences of how we act now.

Although I am certain that what I have seen will come about, I have never felt any conflict between my future visions and a belief in free will. It is rather like looking at life as a giant jigsaw which starts in the foreground (the present) and works up to the sky (the future). Most precognitive experiences are like being given pieces out of sequence – like getting a piece of sky when one is only up to the grass or trees – and these small fragments may only make complete sense as the bigger picture becomes clear. At the time of a vision, I may have no indication of the events occurring on either side of it, but every day we are given more pieces. Perhaps each single choice we make in life causes a particular piece of the future to become inevitable, so that it can be foreseen, while the rest around it is still fluid and mutable. As we fill in the rest of the jigsaw, I believe that we have free will to make choices and decisions that will affect the whole picture, both for the individual and for the planet.

When I started my search to substantiate my future life as Nadia in Nepal, my task seemed to be to locate a probable area and to check the details I had seen for accuracy within obvious limitations. I found what I was looking for with as much success as might be possible. The topography of the area, climate, customs, even the unlikely soil with its reddish tinge, all seemed to be reasonable and accurate. Yet as I continued, the task itself became almost incidental to the emotional and spiritual impact of this journey. Similarly, my continuous monitoring of my further experiences under hypnosis, so necessary to maintain objectivity, did not halt a growing alteration in my attitude. What remained with me was not the importance of any particular events that the future might hold, but a sense of spirit.

We are not isolated in time. Our present is dependent upon our past, and our future on both past and present. One of the things we do at an individual level over the course of time is to learn through experience. We have to make mistakes in order to understand ourselves, and only by taking action can we create change in our lives. We need to know what negative emotions are holding us back before we can let them go in order to develop more positive attitudes. This process can give us the chance to face the future more easily.

If we reincarnate, we can be born again anywhere. This means that currently any oppressive regime, or mistreatment of a minority group for any reason, or localised poverty, should be of concern to us all. If such conditions continue, each of us stands a chance of being born as the victim of oppression at some point.

Tolerance towards others, however different in outlook, background or belief, is a basic ethos of most religious teaching. But in the light of our changing from life to life, during which we might have lived within many cultures and held a variety of beliefs, the meaning and importance of tolerance become even clearer. Tolerance does not consist just of putting up with other people's differences; it is the deep-down realisation that at base none of us is actually different from or better than or even separate from the rest of humanity.

Accepting the concept of reincarnation may help us, too, to understand the importance of both forgiveness and self-forgiveness, and to appreciate that continuing to carry a sense of guilt or resentment can only cause us damage. If we do indeed have the chance to meet up, over and over again, with past-life friends and family members, understanding the sense of continuity can help us to make a better job of our relationships. It may also help us to be patient. We will live more easily with ourselves when we understand that our time is not limited to one life – that there are some things which we cannot hurry and which will only happen when we are ready.

I believe that as individuals we are all affected by the consciousness of the group as a whole. Thus a society may have a group feeling of despair or greed that is damaging to everyone, or indeed a sense of hope and enthusiasm that uplifts the whole group. As individuals, we may not be aware of these influences, but since our future depends on change we need to become aware of them. At this stage in humanity's history we have been making many mistakes in our treatment of the environment, and we are just beginning to learn from them. Rather than despairing about our future, adopting a positive outlook can help to uplift those around us, so that hope itself can become a constructive force in creating our future.

The future that I see looks promising, although there will be problems on the way. If my visions are right, we will have to cope with the legacy of pollution for longer than many people might anticipate. Piecing together the precognitive visions which have occurred over the course of my life with what I have seen under hypnosis, I believe that the next fifty years or so, up to about 2050, will see only a gradual change. The rise in population will slow down and in Western societies the actual numbers may begin to drop. There will be an increase in the toxicity of water, especially of the seas. Diseases such as cancer and those related to newly mutated viruses and bacteria will continue to increase, though slowly enough at first to remain under some control. Problems with flooding due to the greenhouse effect will be quite gradual but persistent.

The most difficult time will probably be over the following hundred years, when the drop in population is becoming marked while levels of pollution and pollution-related disease, including birth defects, are increasing. The average lifespan may even drop for about a fifty-year period, partly due to the increased strain of fighting against the new diseases with immune systems damaged by pollutants and increased radiation from the sun. After that, the birth rate will become markedly reduced.

The population changes caused by infertility will be at their height around two hundred years from now, when the world population will only be a small fraction of its current numbers. At the same time the oceans will have reached a peak of toxicity. But I also see that period two hundred hundred years hence as a turning point. There will be fewer people, but we will have learned from the afflictions of pollution and will have effected change in our interaction with the environment to correct our past mistakes.

If what I have seen is accurate, by the time of Janice's birth around 2190 there seems to be an improvement in living conditions and health, though cancer remains a problem. The quality of life for every person will have become a matter of importance worldwide, in a way that many people might dearly wish were the case now. By this stage the air is very clean though the oceans are still recovering, and the ozone problem seems long forgotten; although the sunlight seems strong, it will not be harmful. This will not be Utopia, but I believe that we will have reached a stage where both the individual and society are respected and work in harmony with each other. For that turning point to arrive, the changes need to start today. As society learns, not only the group but individuals will be affected for the better.

A world seen as one energy, in which there is a balance between all things, is not a new idea. The Native Americans, amongst others, had a very good understanding of their place within the web of life. For centuries they lived in such a way as to minimise their impact on the environment. They would ask the spirits' permission before cutting down a tree or killing an animal, and would only take what they needed; greed was not allowed. They had no concept of the ownership of land, since land could no more be owned by men than could air or water.

This way of understanding nature as a whole and interdependent unit echoes my memory feelings of the between-life period and the feelings of those who have had near-death experiences. Without bodies we consist of pure energy, and that energy seems to be mainly composed of light. Light is the very essence of living energy experienced in the between-life state by those who have had NDEs or past-life memories: virtually all of them have described an experience of vibrant, living light. Frequently people have spoken of beings of light, who are bathed in light, glow with light or who simply are pure light. There are descriptions of rainbow light, sometimes in the form of a colourful garden wound through with sparkling streams, as though various energy frequencies of light exist side by side. Underlying everything is an energy which may be composed of the combined light of the individual energies or may consist of their light together with additional energy. Yet within this realm of energy each person remains individual, separate but connected.

One effect of the reduction in population will be that we will not have to return so rapidly from this realm of light to re-enter a physical body, and a more natural rhythm will be restored to the ebb and flow of these two life states. It is possible that staying longer in the between-life state could mean a greater chance of returning with some of the feelings of love and connectedness involved in that state, making a positive addition to the next physical life and those with whom we interact.

Whatever we experience and learn in that restful between-life state, I am convinced that our role on this planet is one of action and interaction. When we take on physical bodies, the spiritual life is about learning to live in harmony with our environment and with each other. Living a physical life gives us the opportunity to face the demands of living and to grow and learn. All we can do as individuals is to try to understand our role in events, and to try to take the right action at the right time. Our shared responsibility must be to humanity in general.

I look forward with hope and with enthusiasm, willing to face whatever challenges future lives bring forward. Some situations, like the drop in population and the increase in disease, have, I believe, already been set in motion and cannot be avoided. A reduced population can only be for the good. With fewer people there will be less likelihood of hunger, overcrowding, poverty and abuse. In terms of human history a couple of hundred years is not long, but it may be long enough for us to realise some of the things that we need to do to ensure that the world of tomorrow is the kind of world that we could all enjoy living in.

Whatever visions of the future may show, it is a future that includes each one of us. Seeing ourselves and others in the context of time stretching back and forward through history and through many lives can help us to understand our individual roles as interdependent, and our responsibilities as universal. Our attitudes today will make a difference to our future, as individuals and as a society. We can all make tomorrow a place for hope.